continued

A THINK-ALOUD APPROACH TO WRITING ASSESSMENT

Analyzing
Process and Product
with Adolescent Writers

Sarah W. Beck

Foreword by George Newell

TEACHERS COLLEGE PRESS
TEACHERS COLLEGE | COLUMBIA UNIVERSITY
NEW YORK AND LONDON

1234 Amsterdam Avenue
New York, NY 10027-6602

NATIONAL WRITING PROJECT
2105 Bancroft Way
Berkeley, CA 94720-1042

Published by Teachers College Press, 1234 Amsterdam Avenue, New York, NY 10027 and National Writing Project, 2105 Bancroft Way, Berkeley, CA 94720-1042.

Through its mission, the National Writing Project (NWP) focuses the knowledge, expertise, and leadership of our nation's educators on sustained efforts to help youth become successful writers and learners. NWP works in partnership with local writing project sites, located on nearly 200 university and college campuses, to provide high-quality professional development in schools, universities, libraries, museums, and after-school programs. NWP envisions a future where every person is an accomplished writer, engaged learner, and active participant in a digital, interconnected world.

Library of Congress Cataloging-in-Publication Data is available at loc.gov

Names: Beck, Sarah W., author.
Title: A think-aloud approach to writing assessment : analyzing process and product with adolescent writers / Sarah Beck.
Description: New York, NY : Teachers College Press, [2018] | Series: Language and literacy series | Includes bibliographical references and index.
Identifiers: LCCN 2018027381| ISBN 9780807759509 (pbk. : alk. paper) | ISBN 9780807777329 (ebk.)
Subjects: LCSH: Composition (Language arts)—Study and teaching (Middle school) | Composition (Language arts)—Study and teaching (Secondary) | Critical thinking in adolescence.
Classification: LCC LB1631 .B374 2018 | DDC 808/.0420712—dc23
LC record available at https://lccn.loc.gov/2018027381

ISBN 978-0-8077-5950-9 (paper)
ISBN 978-0-8077-7732-9 (ebook)

Printed on acid-free paper
Manufactured in the United States of America

25   24   23   22   21   20   19   18   8   7   6   5   4   3   2   1

Contents

Acknowledgments

Most written texts grow from conversations, and this one is no exception. I am grateful to the many writers and educators who have engaged me in dialogues about the teaching and learning of writing, and literacy more broadly. At New York University, I have been inspired by the intellectual leadership of David Kirkland, who has demonstrated that an active writing life and the relentness pursuit of a better vision for schools and children are not mutually exclusive. Kay Stahl has modeled for me how to link theory and practice in the education of literacy teachers. Audrey Trainor has shown me that it is possible to complete a book-length manuscript while still being a good teacher and citizen. I thank Jasmine Ma for generously sharing her exceptional qualitative toolbench with so many in our community, and for showing me new ways of using the tools within it to understand teacher-student interactions. I owe gratitude to Michael Kieffer for being a constant voice of reason and clarity in all things to do with language and literacy, a voice that I feel has helped sharpen my own. Finally, I am indebted to Lorena Llosa, mentor, coauthor, trusted confidante and friend, who has helped me see critical feedback as a challenge to embrace, and an opportunity for learning and growth. Also at NYU I have been fortunate to collaborate with many talented doctoral students who have assisted me in this work and shaped my understanding of what I could learn from it. Christine Rosalia, Tim Fredrick, Cecilia Zhao, Kristin Black, and Alyssa T. G. Anderson all helped me understand the true potential of the think-aloud as a teaching tool. Gabriel Reich helped me appreciate what thinking aloud can reveal about students' historical understanding. Johanna Tramantano gave me useful perspective on how this individualized method might appeal to district administrators tasked with promoting data-driven instruction. With her unflagging resourcefulness in identifying problems and proposing solutions, and her boundless optimism about life, Karis Jones has been an invaluable collaborator.

Within the broader literacy education community, many have contributed to the expansion of my understanding of how one becomes a writer. Tom Newkirk, Peter Smagorinsky, George Newell, Maureen Barbieri, Mary Juzwik, Amanda Godley, Heidi Andrade, Glynda Hull, Catherine Snow, and Lowry Hemphill deserve particular mention for their timely and productive influence.

I am a student as well as a teacher, and I must thank my guitar instructor, Stephen Z. Becker, for introducing me to the universe of musical composing, the joy and mystery of which I am only beginning to understand, and for thereby renewing my perspective on composing with language.

The process of composing this first book was far from simple and linear. For her encouragement and steadfast belief in the value of the project, I am grateful for the encouragement of Emily Spangler at Teachers College Press, who first saw the potential for a book in this work. In the home stretch of my writing, the manuscript was greatly improved by Myra Cleary's astute and sensitive copyediting.

Emotional support is as essential as intellectual support in the writing of a book. Without the goodwill of my family, I could not have completed this project. I am grateful to my parents, Jay and Carolyn, and my sister, Emily, for understanding that eventually I would be able to fully participate in holiday celebrations and special events. With a finite number of hours in a day, time spent on writing is time not spent on something else, including important household tasks and familial obligations. I thank my husband, Wojtek, for taking on so many of these so that I could have the time I needed, and for understanding why I would want to write a book at all. Finally, I thank my son, Oscar, for the privilege of witnessing him develop as a writer from early childhood to early adolescence. This book is dedicated to him.

Foreword

Teaching writing as "test-prep" is the status quo for English language arts teachers today, and one of the more profound implications of being a student in a test-prep environment is alienation. When during an interview for my own research, I asked a student what he regarded as most valuable about writing, he commented, "Well, I really like to express myself about my ideas and how I think about stuff—like I do when I write at home. But I don't think teachers are always interested in what I have to say. And it's not their fault because they are always worrying about how we'll do on the [writing] tests." Such a remark is understandable given the contexts that high-stakes assessment can create, contexts that are shared by students and teachers alike. The timing of this book could not be better as a catalyst for a counter-movement against such alienation. As I read Sarah Beck's book, I was struck by her efforts to employ think-alouds as a practice that may bring student writers and their readers into profound connection with one another.

Beck demonstrates, in a range of classrooms, how the think-aloud approach to writing assessment allows the teacher to listen carefully and thoughtfully to how students express themselves—or, put another way, how students *language meaning*. As Bloome and Beauchemin (2016) argue, considering *language* as a verb rather than a noun (cf. Becker, 1991) allows us to understand how language-as-action, or "languaging," contributes to personhood—meaning how a culture or subculture (such as a classroom) conceptually defines a "person." Think-aloud writing assessment, as Beck describes it, thus becomes a way for students and teachers to socially construct what it means to be a person and a writer through languaging.

One example of how this can play out appears in the first pages of the book, where we meet Eva and her teacher engaging in a think-aloud as Eva composes an argumentative essay based on *Jane Eyre*, a novel her teacher, Ms. March, had assigned in class:

> *Eva:* I was saying then she moved to school, but I didn't write why she moved to other school because the aunt didn't take care of her. Then she went to school to learn how to read and write. She met friend. Her name is Helen. I forgot the teacher name.
> *Ms. March:* Just do your best.
> *Eva:* Then she became—become a teacher on the school.

Eva continues writing
Ms. March: What are you thinking about, Eva?

The think-aloud assessment method allows Eva to language ("I was saying") her first draft within the presence of Ms. March, who seems to engage Eva as a person with her own ideas and experiences to draw upon as she makes her argument. The open-ended prompt that she offers—"What are you thinking about, Eva?"—is a cornerstone of the think-aloud method, designed to allow students like Eva to discover their ideas about the novel. But this prompt, and the interaction as a whole, allow Eva and Ms. March to language a relationship with one another. In a follow-up interview, reflecting on this conversation, Ms. March describes how the conversation allowed her to notice a divide between Eva's "complex thinking and much simpler writing. . . . I don't think I realized how deep that divide is because it's hard in a class with 30 to really know how much she understands."

While Beck's knowledge as a teacher and scholar of written composition is on full display, her argument for the value of thinking aloud as assessment also provides the field in general and practitioners in particular with a new vision of formative assessment. When a teacher listens carefully to a student's sense-making, assessment becomes a formative process of languaging understanding rather than determining a rationale for a grade. Rather than imposing the positions of observer and observed on teacher and student, Beck's approach to assessment illustrates how, through languaging, they can construct a relationship of care, support, and mutual understanding. It is inherent in the relational model of formative assessment that Sarah Beck introduces us to that teachers become conscious of how their practices contribute to the construction of "persons" as writers in their classrooms.

—George Newell

REFERENCES

Becker, A. L. (1991). Language and languaging. *Language & Communication*, 11, 33–35.

Bloome, D., & Beauchemin, F. (2016). Languaging everyday life in classrooms. *Literacy Research: Theory, Method, and Practice*, 65(1), 152–165.

CHAPTER 1

Introduction

Thinking Aloud as an Assessment Opportunity

All that the children write, your response to what they write, their response to each other, all this takes place afloat upon a sea of talk. (Britton, 1970, p. 29)

Eva, a 10th-grade English learner, is composing an essay about *Jane Eyre*. She has been asked to choose a book and write an essay arguing why it is a good and important book to read. She read *Jane Eyre* in her ESL class; the teacher assigned it because it is a canonical book that will help prepare students for the state exam that Eva will have to pass if she is to graduate from high school. Ms. March, her teacher, listens and observes Eva writing and thinking out loud as she composes. Here is one excerpt from their interaction:

Eva: I was saying then she moved to school, but I didn't write why she moved to other school because the aunt didn't take care of her. Then she went to school to learn how to read and write. She met friend. Her name is Helen. I forgot the teacher name.
Ms. March: Just do your best.
Eva: Then she became—become a teacher on the school.
Eva continues writing. More than 30 seconds pass before Ms. March prompts Eva to speak:
Ms. March: What are you thinking about, Eva?
Eva: That she doesn't like it, but she want to be a teacher. But she doesn't like to work in that school. She don't like it from the first place. Maybe that's why she came to move—I mean, she went to teach in the house. I think she choose to be a teacher at the house because she doesn't like the school.
Eva continues writing.
Ms. March: What are you thinking about?
Eva: When she moved to that house, she find them different from her. They are a higher level, and she's a lower level, so she have to find different—a hard time. But still she liked the place, and she liked the people who lived there. And she liked them more than she likes school.

Immediately after Eva finished this session, Ms. March spoke with an interviewer about what she learned from observing and listening to Eva work through this writing task. She reflected:

> The thing I noticed [in her speaking] is that she creates a lot of complex sentences which I hadn't really thought about. . . . She does a lot of contrasting, which is surprising as her level of language proficiency isn't that strong. So there's this complex thinking and much simpler writing. . . . I don't think I realized how deep that divide is because it's hard in a class with 30 to really know how much she understands.

The above illustrates a writing assessment based on the *think-aloud protocol*, a research method that has been used to study expertise in a wide array of disciplines as well as in writing (Bereiter, Burtis, & Scardamalia, 1988; Flower & Hayes, 1981). In this approach, students verbalize their thoughts as they compose a piece of writing, while the teacher listens, observes, and takes systematic notes on a student's work. In contrast to the more typical writing assessment based on what's written on paper, writing assessment with the think-aloud protocol requires students to verbalize their internal thought processes as they compose, making these processes visible to the teacher and to the students themselves. In this way, it highlights places where students may encounter obstacles, such as interpreting the writing task, generating ideas for their writing, organizing their writing, or meeting particular requirements of a genre—for example, finding relevant evidence for a literary argumentation task. When the teacher employs a systematic method of record-keeping to take note of what she notices in the students' verbalized thoughts or observes in their affect, posture, and behavior, she gains information that allows her to say more than "this student has trouble with thesis statements" or "this student doesn't seem to understand how to analyze characters." The teacher may learn, for example, that the student really doesn't understand the requirements for a thesis statement in the assigned genre, or that, as shown in the example of Eva, the student does have an understanding of characters' motivation, even if that understanding does not come across clearly in the student's writing.

Another likely benefit of using the think-aloud approach is that a teacher will pay more attention to students' strengths as writers (Beck, Llosa, Black, & Trzeszkowski-Giese, 2015), thereby shifting the emphasis of writing assessment toward learning and development (Stiggins, 2001). In the example above, listening to Eva verbalize her thinking process as she composed an essay about a challenging source text—a 19th-century novel, no less—allowed Ms. March to discern Eva's level of comprehension and ability to construct sentences. Prior to conducting this assessment activity with Eva, Ms. March had seen her writing as limited and simplistic, and had assumed her understanding of the texts the class was writing about was the same. After the assessment, however, she was able to recognize new skills and levels of comprehension in Eva's analysis.

In this book I will discuss how teachers can use think-aloud writing assessment to understand, with nuance and precision, the strengths and challenges of student writers. I will propose a conceptual framework, *dialogic writing assessment*, to account for the unique characteristics and affordances of the think-aloud method as a type of formative writing assessment. I will offer suggestions for ways that teachers can support students' writing processes in an interactive version of the think-aloud, described in Chapter 2, by providing feedback that responds to students' challenges in ways that are both more timely and more closely aligned with these challenges. I will share what teachers have learned about students' writing from using this method and will propose how this learning can be a catalyst for collective pedagogical change within professional learning communities (Dufour, 2004). And, because I believe that students should be the ultimate beneficiaries of any writing assessment practices, I will describe what students I have worked with have learned from this method.

This book is based on research I have conducted with teachers over the past several years and with the assistance of several doctoral students and colleagues. The examples of think-aloud sessions that I present to illustrate my suggestions are taken from this research. To give readers some sense of the characteristics of the teachers and students I worked with, in Appendix C, I present a brief summary of the writing assignment each teacher used for the think-aloud assessment. All were high school English language arts (ELA) or ESL teachers, although I encourage teachers of middle school students to consider whether the think-aloud method also may work for them. Many researchers have used the think-aloud with students in the 11–13 age range (Fox, Dinsmore, & Alexander, 2010; Williamson, Carnahan, & Jacobs, 2012) and have found that students are able to think aloud and reflect on their thinking processes in the way that the think-aloud assessment requires.

The potential benefits of using the think-aloud for writing assessment extend beyond the English classroom, because writing with fluency, confidence, and clarity is important not only to the study of literature and language, but also to success in other academic subjects and in post-academic careers. Writing now is assigned in subjects other than English more than it was several decades ago, with large-scale survey research suggesting that the amount of writing that students do in all other subjects combined is greater than the amount assigned in English classes (Applebee & Langer, 2011). Since the adoption of the Common Core State Standards (CCSS) by most states in 2013, teachers in all subjects have been encouraged to use writing as a way of engaging students with subject-matter content; recent surveys reveal that four out of five high school teachers use writing in some way to support learning (Gillespie, Graham, Kiuhara, & Hebert, 2014). And we know that writing about a text contributes to better text comprehension (Marshall, 1987), particularly when students revise that text in response to open-ended, elaboration-prompting questions from a teacher-as-reader (Newell, 1994). The need for methods of assessing writing that have meaningful and immediate instructional impact has never been greater, and think-aloud writing assessment provides a unique context for teachers to understand how students' developing content understanding and their ability to communicate that understanding intersect.

The work that I describe here builds on the influence of esteemed literacy educators and researchers who advocated for the importance of talk to students' writing development: James Britton, Martin Nystrand, Nancie Atwell, and Lucy Calkins. These influential scholars helped generations of teachers understand how central speaking and listening are to effective writing instruction. If our writing assessment practices are to be true to their legacy, then our assessment practice needs to include speaking and listening as well. I hope that readers will find among these pages some practical strategies for using student talk as a window into students' writing processes, and sufficient inspiration to commit themselves to making these strategies a regular element of their writing assessment practice.

INFORMING INSTRUCTION WITH DIAGNOSTIC AND FORMATIVE ASSESSMENT

In order to comprehend how thinking aloud can be effective as a form of writing assessment, it's helpful first to understand how assessment can be used for diagnostic and formative purposes, and how those purposes are different from assessing for writing achievement. If teachers understand what the purpose of an assessment is, they will be better able to interpret the information they get from the assessment in ways that suit that purpose. Writing achievement assessments—the kind to which the general public pays the most attention—are designed for the purpose of determining whether students have met standards and, if not, how far they are from meeting them. Teachers concerned with improving their instruction, and with helping students where they need the most help, probably will be more interested in diagnostic and formative assessments, because their results have direct implications for teaching.

Diagnostic assessments are designed to identify students' challenges with specific areas of knowledge or sets of skills, to illuminate what students do or do not know about a topic, or what they can and cannot do in relation to a specified domain of skill (Ciofalo & Wylie, 2006). Although the medical origin of the word *diagnostic* can suggest an unhelpful connotation of deficiency, the term *diagnostic assessment* also can refer to assessments that identify simply what students have not yet learned (Collins Block, 2003). Diagnostic assessments break down a body of knowledge or domain of skill into separate elements and shed light for teachers, parents, and students on where strengths and challenges lie; they also may illuminate some reasons for these challenges. A number of paper-and-pencil diagnostic writing assessments, such as the Test of Written Language-4 (TOWL-4) (Hammill & Larsen, 2009), are available for teachers to use. These typically employ decontextualized items such as multiple-choice questions or single-sentence tasks that involve sentence combining or sentence correction for problems with grammar, punctuation, or logic. Some, like the TOWL-4, which is probably the most widely used diagnostic assessment of writing, also have an extended writing task in which students compose a response to a prompt that is then scored with a rubric. These extended writing tasks are of necessity limited to one genre (narrative, in the case of the TOWL-4), which may limit the usefulness of the results for middle and high school teachers tasked with improving students' ability to write in analytic, explanatory, and argumentative genres that requires students to synthesize information or write about source text. These types of assessments are efficient to administer to a large group of student and can be useful to teachers because, when results are aggregated across the classroom, they provide an inventory of certain kinds of problems with students' writing—problems with grammar, spelling, vocabulary, and text organization, for example—to help teachers prioritize the focus of their instruction. However, because paper-and-pencil diagnostic writing assessments assess only the product of students' composing, and do not gather information about process, they leave unanswered teachers' questions about the causes of students' difficulties with writing.

While the purpose of diagnostic assessment is to identify difficulties, misconceptions, or gaps in student knowledge, the purpose of formative assessment is to contribute to learning through feedback and improved teaching. For this reason, diagnostic assessments often are used in formative ways. There is more to formative assessment than just informing instruction, however. A comprehensive set of criteria for formative assessment includes the following (Cizek, 2010; Erickson, 2007; Heritage, 2010; Shepard, 2000; Wiliam, 2010):

- It must be aligned with clear learning goals (more on this in Chapter 4).
- These goals must be meaningful in contexts beyond a particular classroom—that is, they must be meaningful in the context of a discipline or general academic literacy practices.
- It provides feedback to learners that is precise and timely, without a long delay.
- It provides students with a sense of their present level of performance and also the steps they need to take to achieve goals.
- It yields information that teachers can, and do, use to plan instruction.
- It includes students as stakeholders and active participants in the assessment process, making grading criteria explicit to students and promoting metacognitive reflection.

Sociocultural theory offers a perspective on formative assessment that is especially student-centered. Lorrie Shepard (2000) argues that to think about assessment in a sociocultural way means to emphasize gaining insight into learners' processes rather than judgmental evaluation of their products, while Pamela Moss (2003) advises us to focus on assessing students' *competence* rather than their *achievement*. This is an important distinction to make because from a sociocultural perspective the reference point for competence is successful participation in a community of practice (Wenger, 1998) that abides by shared norms rather than adhering to a distant, external standard. While classrooms, of course, will be informed by standards such as the CCSS, what matters for classroom assessment when we think in a socio-cultural way, with a focus on student learning, is how we implement those standards in the local context of our classrooms.

DIALOGIC WRITING ASSESSMENT: A CONCEPTUAL FRAMEWORK

As I reviewed the concept of formative assessment through a sociocultur-al lens, it occurred to me that "dialogic assessment" would be an apt way of thinking about formative assessment as it applies to writing. The emphasis on competence within a community of practice—whether a classroom or a school subject, like English—over achievement, and on process over product, is consistent with how the term *dialogic* has been used in research on writing and writing instruction, in several ways:

1. Our ideas as writers are never uniquely our own; they emerge from conversations with other humans and other texts—both in and beyond the classroom. Thinking aloud in the presence of another person enacts the Vygotskian notion that thinking is a social rather than an individual act (Smagorinsky, 1998).
2. All writing has an implied reader. This assumption is central to the dialogic theory of discourse proposed by Mikhail Bakhtin (1986). Possessing awareness of a reader's expectations, and being able to refine that awareness according to genre and communicative purpose, is a hallmark of "competence" as a writer. Developing this awareness is one of the main challenges in learning how to write successfully (Elbow, 1981). By acting as a listener during the student's composing process in dialogic writing assessment, the teacher can develop this awareness.
3. Like dialogic teaching (Juzwik, Borsheim-Black, Caughlan, & Heintz, 2013), dialogic assessment involves talking as a form of learning. For example, by talking, students can discover connections and inconsistencies in their thinking that can inform their writing. Dialogic approaches to learning generally are concerned with *becoming* (Bakhtin, 1986) rather than being, with the direction of development rather than achievement of milestones. Giving the teacher access to the student's thinking-in-process also allows the teacher insight into anything that might need to be unlearned, or any knowledge or skill that might need to be developed, in order for the student's writing to progress.

The think-aloud assessment method that I describe in this book is not the only way to practice dialogic assessment. Any practice of writing assessment that reflects the principles described above could, in my view, be considered dialogic. Nelson Graff's (2009) use of reader think-alouds for peer review, for instance, is an excellent example of another approach to writing assessment that reflects a dialogic orientation. By describing think-aloud writing assessment in terms of this broader framework, I hope to make it possible to link it conceptually to a sociocultural orientation to teaching and learning and make a case for why teachers who align themselves with this orientation would want to practice it.

DIAGNOSTIC AND FORMATIVE POTENTIAL OF THINK-ALOUD WRITING ASSESSMENT

Think-aloud assessment can be seen as both a diagnostic and formative assessment, because of its potential to reveal challenges with writing that paper-and-pencil diagnostic assessments cannot, and because of its close alignment with process-based approaches to writing instruction. Both aspects of the think-aloud's potential can be traced to its original purpose as a research tool.

Speaking While Doing: What Does This Reveal?

The original developers of the think-aloud method were aiming to expand the amount and kind of information that researchers could obtain about human thinking and behavior (Ericsson & Simon, 1993). Psychologists had other tools in their toolbox for studying human performance—such as tracking eye movements, keystrokes on a keyboard, or clicks on a button—but limiting study of human performance to this kind of physical or "nonverbal" data was considered insufficient and, eventually, at odds with the expanded, more complex view of the human mind that developed during the cognitive revolution in the 1950s and 1960s.

In the early 1980s, the think-aloud protocol was taken up by writing researchers who employed the method to study composing processes, investigating differences in composing between expert and novice writers, and in first and second languages (Bereiter & Scardamalia, 1987; Cumming, 1989; Flower & Hayes, 1981). Since then, researchers have used the think-aloud protocol as a research tool to explore whether students use different writing strategies for different genres of writing (Beauvais, Olive, & Passerault, 2011; Durst, 1987) and what is challenging about revision (van Gelderen, 1997). And the protocol has been used extensively to study the unique processes and challenges of second-language (L2) writers, with findings of particular significance for teachers of the growing numbers of English learners (ELs) in schools today. We know from this work, for example, that experience with writing has a greater effect on L2 writers' processes than language proficiency does (Cumming, 1989), and that in general, L2 writers tend to engage in less planning and goal-setting, and in less rereading and reflecting on the texts they have written, than first-language writers do

(Silva, 1993). I myself first used the think-aloud as a research tool to investigate high school students' difficulties with argumentative writing, in collaboration with some colleagues (Beck, Llosa, & Fredrick, 2013). When we saw how much detail our student participants were able to provide about their writing process, even with minimal training, and the extent to which they revealed challenges with interpreting the writing tasks, anticipating audience concerns, and analyzing source texts, it occurred to us that thinking aloud could be useful as an assessment tool. Our intuition was supported by findings from reading comprehension researchers who studied think-alouds as reading assessments (Caldwell & Leslie, 2010), finding that this method provided different information from the typical retelling method of reading assessment.

Does speaking while thinking about a problem or task affect how one works on the task? A reasonable question to ask, since as teachers we don't want to add more complexity to the already challenging task of writing. Fortunately for us, we can find some answers from researchers who have investigated this question directly and discovered that when people are asked to introspect and explain their thinking, it can have a positive effect on performance (Ericsson, 2003). For example, explanatory thinking aloud improved students' understanding of science texts (Chi, de Leeuw, Chiu, & LaVancher, 1994). In a similar way, thinking aloud while writing can improve students' understanding of their own writing processes, fostering greater metacognition and a stronger sense of self-efficacy. In this way, thinking aloud can have an instructional effect. Assessment that involves thinking aloud can integrate assessment and instruction in the same activity, thereby contributing to the formative characteristics of the think-aloud assessment. Finally, speaking aloud while writing can foster a keener sense of what written language sounds like. The author C. S. Lewis gave this advice to writers: "Always write with the ear, not the eye. You should hear every sentence you write as if it were being read aloud or spoken" (quoted in Murray, 1990, p. 134). In the same way that students can be taught to have an ear for music, think-aloud writing assessment can help students develop their ear for writing.

Think-Aloud Assessment and the Writing Process

The think-aloud method of assessing writing is aligned with process-based, authentic models of writing instruction in several ways. First, as a dialogic method of writing assessment, it positions the teacher as an audience for the student's writing, highlighting for students the presence of a reader and the inherent *addressivity* of all texts (Bakhtin, 1986). Second, a teacher who uses think-aloud assessment should assume that the thoughts a student verbalizes while composing are inherently tentative, often preceding a commitment to writing something on the page (although students often do verbalize language as they are writing it down). Such tentativeness is to be encouraged and cultivated; it is like the "inner speech" that Vygotsky argued was a rehearsal for articulating thoughts in standardized, conventional, and complete utterances.

According to Vygotsky (1978), inner speech is a primary means by which *internalization of psychological processes* occurs, when learners repeat language or ideas that they have heard in discourse with teachers, other adults, or more experienced learners, and eventually assimilate this language for use in their own thinking. As Peter Smagorinsky (1998) claimed, when characterizing the think-aloud protocol as a tool for exploring sociocultural aspects of thinking, speaking inevitably shapes thought: "The processes of rendering thinking into speech is not simply a matter of memory retrieval, but a process through which thinking reaches a new level of articulation" (p. 173).

Third, as an assessment method aligned with process models of writing, the think-aloud assessment has diagnostic potential in that it can provide nuanced information about the nature of students' challenges with writing. Janet Emig (1971), who was one of the first to use a think-aloud method to study high school students' writing processes, argued that teachers "underconceptualize and oversimplify" (p. 98) the process of composing, and that most students need "constant and specific guidance" (p. 99) from their teachers to translate into practice abstract concepts such as conciseness, clarity, and depth of writing. By making these goals for writing instruction visible in all their nuance and complexity, the think-aloud writing assessment allows teachers to characterize students' challenges with more precision.

Fourth, focusing assessment on the writing process also allows writing assessment to be more individualized. Peter Elbow (1973), Donald Murray (1968), and Donald Graves (1982) highlighted the need for student writers to find their own unique voices and approaches to writing. Earlier I discussed how including students as agentive stakeholders in the assessment process is one principle of sound formative assessment practice. Fostering students' voice and agency in the writing process is a way to enact this principle in a way that is specific to writing. As I will illustrate throughout this book, think-aloud writing assessment can give teachers insight into how a variety of processes can result in strong writing.

Finally, a social, interactive assessment method honors the social nature of the writing process. It is now widely accepted—by researchers who study writing, particularly in academic contexts, and by teachers who write about their practice for teacher readers—that writing is as much a social practice as a cognitive one. One important implication of this social view is that writing should be considered an interaction, "an exchange of meaning or transformation of shared knowledge" (Nystrand, 1989, p. 74). If we assume that writing is always a conversation, then what could be a better assessment method for writing than one grounded in speaking and listening?

Using Diagnostic Information to Inform Instruction

Above I've discussed reasons why teachers are likely to find the think-aloud assessment method useful for identifying students' strengths and challenges with writing so that they can develop instruction to emphasize the former and address the latter. Now I will review briefly what makes think-aloud writing assessment well suited to informing instruction and promoting student ownership and agency in writing—both key characteristics of formative assessment.

First, it is flexible and not prescriptive: teachers can customize any version of this approach to align with their particular goals at any given time. This customization may happen with respect to the type of writing task teachers design (more on this below) and what they choose to observe and take note of for record-keeping (more on this below), and/or with respect to the prompts and questions teachers design in the interactive version of the assessment (more on this in Chapter 2).

Second, because it can provide detailed and nuanced information about students' writing processes, it offers a range of possible focal points for instruction. I will elaborate further on this point in Chapters 3 and 4. For now, I will note that because think-aloud assessment makes writers' composing processes visible to the teacher and students, and available for reflection and analysis, any aspect of that process may be identified as a source of problems or as a resource for student writers.

Third, because the think-aloud assessment is conducted individually, the teacher can give feedback to students either during the assessment (in the interactive version) or immediately following the session, incorporating the feedback that is essential to formative assessment.

Fourth, think-aloud assessment involves students as stakeholders in their own learning, heightening their sense of self-efficacy as learners and clarifying their sense of their own strengths and challenges as writers. Research suggests that thinking aloud while completing literacy tasks—reading as well as writing—can foster metacognitive skills and self-regulation, both for English monolinguals (Ebner & Ehri, 2013; Kymes, 2005) and for English learners (McKeown & Gentilucci, 2007). Chapter 5 is devoted to a discussion of what students can learn from think-aloud assessment.

SETTING THE STAGE FOR THINK-ALOUD WRITING ASSESSMENT

In the sections above, I characterized think-aloud writing assessment as a dialogic assessment, meaning that it focuses on process rather than product, on the student's development as a writer, and on the social context of authentic communication. In the remainder of this chapter, I will use these characteristics as reference points for explaining how teachers can go about implementing think-aloud assessment in a manner that is most appropriate for their students and their instructional goals.

Preparing Students

In order to assess writing process, teachers need to help students become comfortable and feel safe in verbalizing incomplete, unfinished thoughts.

Although it is not normal or routine for most people, even professional writers, to speak their thoughts while writing, I have encountered students who say that they typically like to talk through their ideas out loud immediately before or as they are writing; not surprisingly, these students take easily to the think-aloud method and tend to produce fluent and complex verbal reports. How can a teacher who wants to implement think-aloud writing assessment help students feel comfortable with the teacher's observation of their process? Teachers can make a habit of modeling their own thinking aloud for students—an instructional practice that frequently is recommended in practitioner guides to reading instruction (e.g., Beers, 2006; Schoenbach, Greenleaf, Cziko, & Hurwitz, 1999). Doing so will help make thinking aloud seem more natural and less intimidating to students, routinizing it as a classroom practice; since the teacher has already taken the risk of sharing his or her thoughts aloud, it may make the activity seem less risky to students. Modeling thinking aloud also may give students some idea of what more experienced writers do when they compose; in fact, this is the underlying rationale for the use of think-aloud as an instructional strategy in cognitive apprenticeship models of teaching literacy (e.g., Schoenbach, Greenleaf , Cziko & Hurwitz, 1999). A cognitive apprenticeship model of learning (Brown, Collins, & Duguid, 1989) is a promising way to prepare a community of students to make productive use of this kind of assessment method. Such apprenticeship-based models of teaching include:

1. explicit depictions by the teacher and other relative experts of the cognitive strategies and metacognitive reflections that constitute expertise in reading and/or writing;
2. the scaffolding of strategy use and reflection with targeted instructional support; and
3. the assumption that novices can and will acquire expert skills and knowledge through structured and sustained work alongside more-expert practitioners of those skills. This socioculturally based approach to classroom assessment assumes that preparing students for an assessment task is not an individual project but rather a collective one.

Such an approach is one way to take up the training that researchers using the think-aloud method have employed in an attempt to make this method seem less artificial. The think-aloud method requires students to be able to introspect—to explain and reflect on their thoughts. Training is especially important for think-aloud tasks that involve introspection rather than simply reporting thoughts (Ericsson & Simon, 1993). To lay a foundation for effective use of the think-aloud writing assessment, explanation and reflection on writing processes should become routine practices in the classroom. When teachers model descriptive and explanatory talk as they demonstrate metacognitive processes, they can support students in becoming better at producing descriptive and explanatory talk in their think-aloud assessments. This is a desirable outcome, given that descriptive and explanatory think-alouds actually have been associated with higher performance on tasks (Fox, Ericsson, & Best, 2011). Training for the assessment becomes intertwined with instruction, exemplifying formative assessment for learning (cf. Stiggins, 2001).

Whether a teacher uses think-aloud assessment in the interactive (described in Chapter 2) or noninteractive way, the method requires that students verbalize their thoughts while composing, attempting as much as possible to say out loud any thoughts that come to mind while crafting a response to a prompt or task. There are a variety of ways that the teacher can support a student in doing this across a broad spectrum of degrees of structure and intervention. At the pole of least intervention, the teacher would say only, "I want you to work on the writing assignment I have given you, and while you are doing this, say what is going through your mind as you write." The teacher then says nothing else other than "remember to say what is going through your mind as you think about what to write," if the student is silent for more than a few seconds. A somewhat more structured version of this nondirective method has the teacher pausing the student at prespecified intervals of the process—for example, after the student has read each sentence of the prompt, or after he or she has written each sentence—but again, not asking any specific questions or prompting a specific kind of thinking, just reminding the student to speak. From there, it is possible to insert questions and prompts of ascending degrees of directiveness, as mentioned above.

It is important to remember that anything counts as part of the writing process once the teacher has asked the student to start thinking about the writing task, even if it seems "off task" or isn't actual writing. Some of the teachers I have worked with have encouraged students to reread portions of the text they are writing about, or their notes on the text, or completed graphic organizers during the think-aloud sessions. All of these activities count as part of the student's unique writing process, and all could be potentially useful and relevant information to note in the record from the think-aloud session.

Setting the Writing Task

The writing tasks used for think-aloud assessment should be aligned with the teacher's curriculum and should represent what authentic performance looks like in the subject the students are learning (Shepard, 2000). What kinds of processes can be considered relevant to these tasks? If we consider that experienced writers often work on a piece of writing mentally even when they are not in front of a computer, or with pen and paper, other activities besides composing words may "count" as part of the process and therefore can be useful to assess. For example, in writing a literary analysis essay, the student needs to generate a thesis idea that is defensible and that makes sense as an interpretation of a literary work, and then needs to be able to select text examples that are relevant and useful in supporting this thesis. An important part of generating content to write about involves reading and interpreting the literary text;

therefore, having students think aloud while close reading a text, or reviewing their notes on a text, may be appropriate for a think-aloud writing assessment session focused on a literary analysis task. In Chapter 4, I say more about how to align think-aloud assessment with instructional goals, and go into more depth about task selection. Defining goals is a prerequisite for understanding the developmental trajectory of a student writer, as every trajectory aims toward an endpoint.

Record-Keeping and Documentation

If teachers and students are to use an assessment as a reference point to determine the next steps in development and plans for instruction, they need a systematic and efficient method of documenting what a student says and does during a think-aloud writing assessment session. The record-keeping method should be customized to match the characteristics of the task. Figure 1.1 is an example of the record-keeping sheet that we gave teachers in our first study of think-aloud writing assessment, which used an argumentative writing task. Figure 1.2 is a template that teachers can use to construct a similar record-keeping tool for their own assignments.

I've included our version of the record-keeping sheet here to give readers a sense of what a complete record-keeping sheet looks like. Perhaps the most important thing to note about this record-keeping sheet is its focus on *process* rather than the written product. The questions contain active verbs rather than nouns—for example, "Does the student *choose* . . . ?" "Does the student *engage* . . . ?" "Does the student *come up with* . . . ?" This is strikingly different from writing rubrics, which ask the teacher to evaluate the degree to which a particular feature is present, or absent, in a student's writing. Another key feature of this record-keeping sheet is the fact that it contains both checklist items (Yes/No/ Not sure) and, for most of the items, a follow-up, open-ended question. I believe both kinds of questions are important for teachers to use. The checklist items prompt teachers to look for a specific process or feature and to react quickly to its presence; these items facilitate quick and efficient recording. The open-ended questions supplement the closed questions by leaving space for elaboration and the kind of detail that can inform instructional planning. To help teachers construct a version of this template to reflect their own teaching priorities, I've included a blank template with sentence stems, based on the tool that we used but with the important addition of space for noting strengths.

In think-aloud writing assessment, observation, as well as listening, is key. Students' posture, facial expression, and even the fluency of their hand movements as they compose can give teachers insight into students' confidence and attitude toward their work, suggesting affective factors that may either interfere with or support their composing processes (Pajares, 2003). The observational aspect of the think-aloud assessment also affords teachers insight into how well students are able to maintain focus and to manage their writing processes. For example, teachers I have worked with have paid attention to the

Figure 1.1. Sample record-keeping sheet for a think-aloud assessment session of students' writing on the task: Write an essay to persuade someone to read a book or watch a movie

1. Does the student interpret the prompt accurately?	**Yes**	**No**	**Not sure**
What, if any, challenges does the student demonstrate related to interpreting the prompt?			
2. Does the student choose a book or film that he or she has enough to say about?	**Yes**	**No**	**Not sure**
What, if any, challenges does the student demonstrate related to choosing a book/film?			
3. Does the student engage in planning and setting goals to complete the task? (Examples of planning include pre-writing, outlining, note-taking, talking through the ideas)	**Yes**	**No**	**Not sure**
What, if any, challenges does the student demonstrate in planning and setting goals?			
4. Does the student come up with a thesis statement?	**Yes**	**No**	**Not sure**
4a. In composing a thesis statement, what, if any, challenges does the student demonstrate?			
5. Does the student generate support for the thesis?	**Yes**	**No**	**Not sure**
5a. In generating support for the thesis statement, what, if any, challenges does the student demonstrate?			
6. Does the student have trouble recalling information from the book or movie?	**Yes**	**No**	**Not sure**
7. Does the student analyze and/or synthesize information from the book or movie and not just summarize it (to use as evidence to support the thesis)?	**Yes**	**No**	**Not sure**
8. Does the student show awareness of audience? (For example, "This would make the movie sound exciting," "I don't want to give the plot away")	**Yes**	**No**	**Not sure**
8a. What challenges does the student demonstrate in relation to audience awareness?			
9. Does the student develop a structure for the essay? (e.g., multiple paragraphs, intro, conclusion)	**Yes**	**No**	**Not sure**
9a. What, if any, challenges does the student demonstrate in developing the structure of the essay?			
10. Does the student connect ideas effectively? For example, does the student use transitions between paragraphs? Does the student refer to the thesis later in the essay?	**Yes**	**No**	**Not sure**

Figure 1.1. Sample record-keeping sheet for a think-aloud assessment session of students' writing on the task: Write an essay to persuade someone to read a book or watch a movie

10a.	What challenges does the student demonstrate in relation to connecting ideas?			
11.	Does the student evaluate and/or revise his or her own writing?	Yes	No	Not sure
11a.	What, if any, challenges does the student demonstrate relative to evaluating and revising?			
12.	Is the student able to stay focused on the task?	Yes	No	Not sure
13.	Does the student have trouble using conventions of standard written English (e.g., correct spelling, punctuation, grammar)?	Yes	No	Not sure
13a.	What, if any, challenges does the student demonstrate relative to conventions?			
14.	Does the student identify appropriate words to express his or her meaning?	Yes	No	Not sure
14a.	What, if any, challenges does the student demonstrate in identifying appropriate words?			
15.	Does the student get too caught up in sentence-level issues and lose sight of the big picture?	Yes	No	Not sure

Please summarize the main strengths and the main challenges that you observed for the student during this protocol.

What, if any, discrepancies did you notice between the thoughts that the student verbalized and the writing composed?

Based on the information you have gathered here, what kinds of instruction or support would you provide to help this student improve his or her writing?

following: students' facial expressions as an indication of their level of frustration with a task or their enthusiasm about a text; whether they squirm or sigh, indicating restlessness and struggle; and the amount of time they take to make decisions about word choice. Teachers may want to focus on affective aspects of composing, such as confidence and fluency, in their record-keeping. The sentence stems offered in Figure 1.2 may be expanded into statements such as, "Does the student seem confident in his or her ability to solve problems during the composing process?" or "Are the student's posture and position relative to the keyboard (or grip on the pen) conducive to avoiding fatigue while composing?" No matter what the focus of the teacher's recording sheet is, it will be important to make space for jotting down next steps for instruction, to be consistent with the developmental orientation of think-aloud assessment.

Selecting Students to Work With

As an individualized and time-intensive method of assessment, the think-aloud writing assessment approach cannot feasibly be used consistently with an entire class on a regular basis. In my experience, it is most efficient and effective when used with students whose writing progress seems stalled for reasons that are not possible to infer from the usual method of scoring or analyzing students' written work with a rubric or checklist, and/or with students who seem to not be learning skills that a teacher has taught repeatedly. Some of the reasons teachers I have worked with have given for selecting particular students to work with include:

- not understanding why a student can't seem to use written feedback to improve a draft of an essay;
- wanting to know whether and to what extent a student has an analytic understanding of a literary text, as opposed to just literal comprehension of a story;
- wanting to know whether a student is making mental connections that he or she is not putting on paper; and
- generally wanting to know more about what is going on in the mind of a student who works very hard but rarely speaks up in class.

An important consideration when selecting students with whom to use the think-aloud is whether they feel comfortable with the process of verbalizing their thoughts out loud. As I discussed above, there are measures a teacher can implement to make thinking out loud routine and unthreatening. However, even with these measures in place, some students may still be uncomfortable putting emergent thoughts into words in front of an audience, or—thinking out loud or not—may not be enamored of the idea of writing beside a teacher who is observing them. It's important not to press this method on students for whom it may be uncomfortable or threatening. In some cases, video or audio recording students as they write and think out loud may be an alternative way of conducting a think-aloud writing assessment if the teacher is interested mainly in seeing what students can do on their own without prompting. Indeed, the idea of video recording oneself engaged in a complex problem-solving task will not be new to students who are active players of videogames. Video recording one's gaming sessions is now a common practice in the gaming community, with many options available for game-capture software, and certain gamers have attained celebrity-like status for the quality of their performances. This analogy was first pointed out to me by a high school student who participated in my research, as I was explaining the think-aloud methodology to him. (We both agreed, however, that writing videos posted to YouTube were unlikely to garner many followers!)

Figure 1.2. Template for designing a record-keeping sheet for think-aloud writing assessment

1. Does the student . . . ?	Yes	No	Not sure
Challenges the student demonstrates related to . . . ?	Strengths the student demonstrates related to . . . ?		
2. Does the student . . . .?	Yes	No	Not sure
Challenges the student demonstrates related to . . . ?	Strengths the student demonstrates related to . . . ?		
3. Does the student engage in . . . ?	Yes	No	Not sure
Challenges the student demonstrates related to . . . ?	Strengths the student demonstrates related to . . . ?		
4. Does the student . . . ?	Yes	No	Not sure
Challenges the student demonstrates related to . . . ?	Strengths the student demonstrates related to . . . ?		
5. Does the student . . . ?	Yes	No	Not sure
In doing . . . what challenges does the student demonstrate?	In doing . . . what strengths does the student demonstrate?		
6. Does the student . . . ?	Yes	No	Not sure
Challenges the student demonstrates related to . . . ?	Strengths the student demonstrates related to . . . ?		

Summarize the main strengths and the main challenges that you observed for the student during this think-aloud protocol:

Strengths:

Challenges:

What are the instructional next steps for this student and others like him or her?

Another potentially useful application of the think-aloud approach is to assess a particular student's strengths to gain insight into what could be taught to or modeled for students who struggle with a specific aspect of writing. For example, a teacher who finds that many students are having difficulty mastering essay structure could select one student who is exceptionally good at organizing essays with whom to conduct a brief think-aloud writing assessment focused on that student's planning and outlining processes. This could give some insight into how the student thinks about planning, and the teacher could then design a lesson that models this strategy.

For guidance on how to select students for think-aloud assessment, teachers could use standardized writing assessment scores or data from interim assessments (assessments periodically administered to track progress toward learning goals) if their school or district has an interim assessment plan. This would allow teachers to link the think-aloud assessment to a larger school-level project in enhancing literacy achievement, as with data inquiry teams. Using large-scale quantitative assessment data as a starting point and background for selecting individual students who represent typical profiles of learning challenges, and then engaging in in-depth qualitative studies of those students, is a reliable formula for reshaping instruction to address student needs (Langer & Colton, 2005).

Special Considerations for English Learners

In addition to the social and emotional factors that teachers need to consider when selecting students to work with in think-aloud writing assessment, language proficiency is an important concern. Research on best practices in teaching writing to English learners points to the important role that regular, frequent formative assessments play in developing English learners' writing skills through practice and consistent feedback (Olson, Scarcella, & Matuchniak, 2015). As I will discuss in more detail in Chapter 3, think-aloud writing assessment can shed unique and useful insights into the writing challenges and strengths of language learners/emergent bilinguals. However, if students are not at least at roughly an intermediate level (e.g., "Transitioning" on the New York State English as a Second Language Achievement Test or "Emerging" on the WIDA performance standards), the task of verbalizing their thoughts in any language other than their native one may prove too challenging and may end up completely derailing the writing process.

Such an outcome is an example of what researchers who employ the think-aloud methodology call *reactivity*—the idea that thinking out loud while completing a task changes the learner's performance on the task—a concern that I discussed earlier in this chapter. Creating a habitual practice of encouraging think-alouds as a teaching method can help mitigate the possibility of reactivity—for all students, not only English learners. Research on the extent to which participants' performance on a writing task was altered by thinking aloud in a language other than their native tongue while completing the task showed that even a metacognitive think-aloud task—in which participants were asked to explain what they were doing and not merely report their thoughts—did not affect participants' production of writing. Importantly, in this particular study, the participants were allowed to use either their first or second language when verbalizing their thoughts (Bowles, 2010).

With this research as background, I recommend that English learners/emergent bilinguals be encouraged to employ their native language—or any other language in which expressing their thoughts comes naturally to them, if they have more than two languages in their repertoires. This is not only to make students feel more comfortable with the task, but also to help them see their native language as a resource and to promote what is known as *additive bilingualism* (Cummins, 1984). As scholars of language education have noted (e.g., Bartlett & Garcia, 2011; Valdes, 2001), U.S. schools have a tendency to view language-minority students' first languages as deficits to be overcome rather than resources to be drawn upon. Yet several influential literacy researchers have argued, based on their own empirical work with language learners in classrooms, that language learners should be given the opportunity to write in their first languages (L1s) as a way of developing their ideas (Ortmeier-Hooper, 2013) and demonstrating the writing abilities that they have practiced and mastered in their L1 (Fu, 2009). Teachers who are not proficient in their students' native languages may feel hesitant to assess any activities where this language is employed, because they believe they are not qualified to assess the language used. However, this need not be a concern. If we agree that student agency and involvement are key characteristics of classroom assessment with formative potential—as Rick Stiggins (2001) and Heidi Andrade (2010) suggest—then we should trust and expect students to be able to explain and reflect on their use of the L1 as a resource for making meaning. Even when they don't understand the words a student is speaking, teachers can note at what point(s) in the composing process the student shifted to his or her L1, and can ask the student after the think-aloud is completed to reflect on why he or she made that linguistic shift. If the think-aloud assessment is audio or video recorded, teachers can even replay that segment for the student to listen to and reflect on. It also may be that a student has very limited English and prefers to think aloud only in the L1. In either case, the teacher could consider recruiting another student with the same L1 as a language broker to interpret the focal student's processes. This is a promising approach given that language brokering has been shown to expand the range of expertise that multilingual students can develop in writing classrooms (Kibler, 2010).

Recording a think-aloud can serve at least two purposes: First, it can serve as an archive of ideas and grammatical formulations that the student can mine in subsequent composing sessions, and, second, it can provide a context for the student to reflect on his or her language proficiency. It is not uncommon for English learners to find it easier to express an idea in a grammatically correct or sophisticated way in speech than in writing. Recognizing that they have attained a certain level of proficiency orally can help students recognize that, with practice, their writing proficiency can reach the same level. Put another way, reflecting on a recording of their verbalized thought processes can help English learners recognize the outer edges of their zones of proximal development and the direction in which their writing development is headed.

CONCLUSION

Whether used with first- or second-language writers, the think-aloud writing assessment can serve as a useful alternative to more typical methods of assessment that focus on evaluating and analyzing the students' writing with rubrics or other scoring tools. As a formative, dialogic assessment method, it provides nuanced information that will allow a teacher to adjust instruction to meet students' needs (Cizek, 2010) in a manner that is aligned with the social nature of written communication, the writing process, and writing development. There has been a growing recognition that high-stakes assessments deployed for accountability purposes can have negative effects for teaching and learning, such as distorting instruction (Hillocks, 2002; Nichols & Berliner, 2007); limiting the variety of writing tasks and thereby options for students' engagement with writing (McCarthey, 2008); detrimentally impacting teachers' relationships with students (Valli & Buese, 2007); and producing incomplete or inaccurate characterizations of students as writers (Dutro, Selland, & Bien, 2013). As Supovitz (2009) has noted, high-stakes testing has served well as a catalyst for system-level change, but has not yielded information helpful for modifying instruction at the classroom level. Think-aloud writing assessment can help address this gap.

CHAPTER 2

Interacting with Students in Think-Aloud Writing Assessment

When I first studied how teachers used the think-aloud method with their students, I presented it to them as a monologic activity, meaning that the goal was to elicit as much talking as possible from students, and to have this talk be minimally influenced by students' concerns about how the teacher was evaluating their ideas or what they thought the teacher wanted to hear. But there are two reasons to question this idealistic view of the potential assessment benefits of uninterrupted thinking aloud. First, it may not be realistic to expect most adolescent students to be comfortable verbalizing their thoughts without feedback from the teacher. Teaching and learning activities in most ELA classrooms are built on the assumption of constant feedback. The ubiquitous I-R-E/I-R-F classroom discourse structure (Mehan, 1979) is just one example of how this assumption plays out every day in classroom interaction. Second, teachers *want* to intervene—and not always because they feel obligated to give feedback or evaluate students' thinking. In my work with that first group of teachers, several of them told me in our debriefing interviews that while they did gain useful information from just listening, they thought they would have learned even more by asking strategic questions. They could have asked, for example, how students were conceptualizing the writing task set for them, what kinds of genre knowledge was coming into play, and whether students were able to access other kinds of important background information, such as interpretive inferences about a literary work if the writing task was in the genre of literary analysis.

This feedback recalls an assertion that Peter Elbow (1987) made in one of his writings about audience:

> Children, and even adults who have not learned the art of quiet, thoughtful, inner reflection, are often unable to get much cognitive action going in their heads unless there are other people present to have action *with*. They are dependent on live audience and the social dimension to get their discourse rolling or to get their thinking off the ground. (p. 56, emphasis in the original)

Ironically, he included this assertion in an article that exhorts writers to try to ignore audience while composing, in order to find their true voices and figure out what they really think about something. This statement echoes the Vygotskian idea that the kinds of cognitive processes involved in composing written text—such as planning, generating ideas in the complex grammar of written text, and synthesizing ideas from multiple sources and from memory —all come into the mind through the experience of social interaction. This is what Peter Smagorinsky (2011) means when he suggests that thinking aloud while writing enables the formation of ideas one would not have without speaking. I used this idea in Chapter 1 to advocate for the idea of dialogic writing assessment as an especially apt way to conceptualize formative assessment of writing. Think-aloud writing assessment exemplifies this idea: Whether the teacher interacts with the student or not, the teacher's presence in either version of the assessment is what makes the assessment dialogic. In the interactive version, however, the dialogue is made explicit because the teacher-listener responds.

ENACTING DIALOGUE THROUGH INTERACTION

Because a dialogic view of writing assessment assumes that writing is inherently a social activity, it invites us to ponder the relationship between writing and speaking. In some ways, the relationship between writing and speaking is a close one. Speaking directly to an audience can lubricate the gears of composition when they are stuck. Many writers, even very experienced and accomplished ones, will resort to talking through their ideas with themselves or a trusted peer when they find themselves at an impasse in their composing processes. And we know that the quality of classroom discussion can have an effect on the quality of students' writing: When teachers ask more dialogic questions—that is, questions that don't have a fixed answer but signal the teacher's authentic interest in students' ideas and interpretations—students tend to write better essays (Nystrand, 1997).

Yet in other ways, writing and speaking are polar opposites: Students who compose academic essays in informal registers or social vernaculars are likely to find their ideas poorly received and may struggle to articulate the kinds of intricate analytic thoughts that characterize academic prose (Schleppegrell, 2004). The challenge for teachers, with regard to helping students navigate the complex relationship between speech and writing, is to help students use spoken language as a resource for developing knowledge while also understanding its distinctness from written language. Interactive think-aloud writing assessment gives teachers an opportunity to assess students' present knowledge about written language and their understanding of the content they are writing about, while also supporting them in developing this understanding. To understand how it is possible for teachers to both assess and instruct students in one activity, we need to consider the tradition of dynamic assessment, an interactive approach to individual assessment that represents a radical departure from standardized, norm-referenced models and that has been developed and applied across a variety of contexts, often with exceptional or vulnerable populations.

THE LEGACY OF DYNAMIC ASSESSMENT

Dynamic assessment emerged as a repudiation of static conceptions of such traits as intelligence and ability, and the related objectives of classifying and sorting students into prescriptive and limiting educational trajectories (Haywood & Tzuriel, 2002). What this tradition shares with dialogic views of writing is a foundation in Vygotsky's notion that learning and development are first and foremost social activities. The interdependence of learning and social interaction is best exemplified in the concept of the *zone of proximal development* (ZPD), "the distance between the actual developmental level as determined by independent problem-solving and the level of potential development as determined through problem-solving under adult guidance or in collaboration with more capable peers" (Vygotsky, 1978, p. 86).

Related to the concept of the ZPD is the notion of mediation, the process by which human thinking is shaped by the influence of other people, physical objects, social processes, or symbolic systems such as language. As applied in dynamic assessment of writing, mediation "refers to the intentional and reciprocal interaction between a tutor (and/or written texts) and the learner in relation to the problems experienced by the learner and the developmental support given by the tutor" (Shrestha & Coffin, 2012, p. 57). Mediation both makes visible the range of the ZPD for any given learner and allows the learner to work within that zone.

The ideas of mediation and the ZPD underlie two key characteristics of dynamic assessment: (1) the assessor deliberately attempts to teach the subject a skill that will improve the subject's performance, and (2) the assessor provides degrees of support that vary depending on the needs of the student, as identified prior to and during the assessment (Haywood, 1992; Haywood & Lidz, 2007). In these ways, dynamic assessment integrates assessment and instruction into one activity, incorporating feedback as an instructional practice (Hattie & Timperley, 2007) and potentially contributing to the development of a culture of learning around assessment (Shepard, 2000). What this means for interaction in think-aloud writing assessment is that when a teacher asks a question or offers a prompt to assess a student's knowledge about writing or a particular writing skill, the teacher also may be providing instructional support that moves the student along in his or her writing.

This is a crucial difference between think-aloud writing assessment and other types of formative assessment, in which the instruction intended to address gaps or difficulties that the assessment has uncovered, is provided after some time has elapsed. An important implication of this difference is that while interactive think-aloud writing assessment is time-intensive for teachers, it has the advantage of offering an opportunity for immediate instruction.

An example from Ms. Schnader's 10th-grade classroom shows how this can occur. Ms. Schnader's students are writing an essay on *Othello* that requires them to make a claim about Othello's character in a central idea (thesis) and support it with evidence. Leslie has composed her thesis about Othello —*the main reason he changed was because he became jealous. Jealousy made him an evil man who became insecure and spiteful*—and is now working on supporting that thesis with the example of Othello's anger over Desdemona losing her handkerchief:

> *Leslie:* Othello . . . became . . . angry . . . when . . . she said . . . she lost it . . . because it was passed down . . . from his mother . . . and it was special . . . to him.
>
> *Ms. Schnader:* Is that the . . . the only reason why he's angry?
>
> *Leslie:* Yeah, because he figures she left it at . . . her . . . relationship's house.
>
> *Ms. Schnader:* Lover's house.
>
> *Leslie:* Yeah.
>
> *Ms. Schnader:* All right. So, do you think that analyzes how his characterization connects to the central idea?
>
> *Leslie:* Yeah, because once he became jealous, he then became insecure and spiteful.
>
> *Ms. Schnader:* Okay. Did you talk about being insecure?
>
> *Leslie:* No.

Ms. Schnader asks Leslie three assessment questions: (1) Is that the only reason he is angry? (2) Do you think that analyzes how his characterization connects to the central idea? and (3) Did you talk about being insecure? These are intended to assess the extent to which the student understands the handkerchief example as being a good choice to support her thesis, and the student's responses show that she does understand. The third question about Othello's insecurity prompts the student to recognize that she has not yet addressed that part of the central idea, and she promptly addresses that problem by adding this sentence to her essay: *Othello then became insecure because of what Iago told him and he didn't want Desdemona sleeping with anyone else.*

Just as interactions in dynamic assessment can foreground either assessment or instruction, they also can foreground either task-specific or general goals. In their study of dynamic assessment of foreign language reading comprehension, Poehner and van Compernolle (2011) invoke these two possibilities when they distinguish between "collaborative" and "cooperative" ways that teachers and learners may interact in dynamic assessment. In collaborative interactions, the focus is more on the process of completing the task at hand, and the tutor works to support the learner by providing exactly the kinds of support needed to complete the task. In cooperative interactional frames, which Poehner and van Compernolle view as more conducive to learner development, teacher and student "move beyond the confines of the immediate task and turn to questions or problems that, while not central to the task, serve to promote learner knowledge and understanding" (p. 193) because they relate to concepts and problems presumably transferrable to other contexts. Although to my knowledge no research exists to prove that cooperative interactions have greater long-term impact on students' learning, I recommend that teachers consider these two possibilities as ways of structuring their interactions with students. As I'll show with the following examples, these frames can be combined in a think-aloud session with a student; it depends on what opportunities arise for thinking more collaboratively or more cooperatively. In the first example, Mr. Tancredi is working with Cameron on an essay about "The Rime of the Ancient Mariner." He initiates the session with a question about time management, and a cooperative type of exchange occurs, in which Mr. Tancredi offers Cameron advice about how to manage his writing process more effectively:

> *Mr. Tancredi:* The very first thing I want to ask you about is your time management. Do you feel that as you were writing, you optimized the use of your time?
>
> *Cameron:* Could you explain optimize for me?
>
> *Mr. Tancredi:* All right. So, different steps through writing process, right? We read the question. We brainstorm. We look for evidence. We organize our ideas. We start writing. Then eventually, revision, which is what we're starting today. Do you feel you were able to manage the time?
>
> *Cameron:* No, not really. In certain areas, I spent more time than other areas. Like starting. I spent the most time on like my first, my opening sentences. But after my opening sentences, everything really comes more easier.
>
> *Mr. Tancredi:* Okay. So, it's that first, first sentence. But there's always the possibility that you could skip your first sentence and start writing. Is that possible for you, you think?
>
> *Cameron:* No, I don't like it, because I like to do things in order.
>
> *Mr. Tancredi:* Okay. So, I can easily give you a checklist of the writing process. It's something I would say is circular. It's actually not this horizontal list but rather a circular list that you're going back and forth and back and forth and back and forth. So, one minute you're writing, the next minute you're revising, the next minute you're doing your first sentence again.
>
> *Cameron:* Okay.
>
> *Mr. Tancredi:* So, I would experiment with maybe starting when you're stuck and then going back to your first sentence.

A few minutes later in the session, Mr. Tancredi shifts the frame to focus on helping the student support his main point with evidence. He begins by asking Cameron to read aloud the sentence that he has marked in bold type as his main point, which he does:

Cameron: "As a retribution to the mariner unlawfully killing a seabird known as an albatross, he has to suffer supernatural consequences."

Mr. Tancredi: All right, so give me two consequences he had to suffer.

Cameron: The one, when he killed the bird, all his crew members, they, they died.

Mr. Tancredi: Okay.

Cameron: The second one was [pause, 14 seconds]—wasn't it a storm?

Mr. Tancredi: There's a storm that came out of nowhere.

Cameron: Yeah.

Mr. Tancredi: So, let's find these in the text.

These examples show how it is possible to use the interactive think-aloud assessment to work on both short-term and long-term goals with students. In the second excerpt from this session, Mr. Tancredi and the student are focused on the problem of finding examples of consequences of killing the albatross—a problem that is specific to this writing task. But in the dialogue about time management, Mr. Tancredi encourages Cameron to reconsider his typical approach to writing problems—doing things in order—as a way to avoid getting stuck. This is a strategy that a teacher could use for any type of writing task. A potentially productive follow-up focus for a subsequent session, in a case like this, would be to coach the student through an initial draft using this new strategy for writing, to help him experience the benefits of a different approach than "doing things in order."

As a method of assessing language or literacy, dynamic assessment has been applied most widely in foreign language teaching. It has proven to be effective in revealing students' varying levels of mastery of particular language features (Davin, 2013; Lantolf, 2009; van Compernolle & Zhang, 2014), for providing teachers with immediate and nuanced information about students' strengths and challenges as language learners (Meskill, 2010; Poehner & Lantolf, 2010), and for assessing and developing sociolinguistic competence (van Compernolle & Williams, 2012). While dynamic assessment has been used in the context of writing instruction, to my knowledge it has been used only with adult learners—for example, to diagnose adult students' challenges with professional writing (Shrestha & Coffin, 2012) and to develop college students' writing skills (Alavi & Taghizadeh, 2014). It is time for the reach of this promising methodology to be extended to adolescent writers, given the sustained focus on writing skills as an element of subject-area learning (Rainey & Moje, 2012) at the secondary level.

WHAT DOES INTERACTIVE THINK-ALOUD ASSESSMENT LOOK LIKE?

Interactive think-aloud assessment requires more up-front planning than the noninteractive version, because in addition to thinking about what skills, processes, strengths, and challenges to assess, teachers also need to plan how they might want to intervene in the composing process to both support and assess the student. In the planning stage, the teacher analyzes the writing task to be used for the assessment and, first, identifies the skills and knowledge required to complete the assignment successfully, as well as the challenges he or she thinks students are likely to experience with the assignment. The teacher also may include in this list of skills and knowledge some that are not unique to this particular assignment but rather are more general, transferrable writing skills such as "rereads and revises for meaning" or "evaluates own work." Next, the teacher creates a set of questions that he or she could ask in order to discern whether students possess the skills necessary to complete the task, as well as the nature of their challenges. In Figure 2.1, I offer a template for creating the list of skills and related questions.

To help teachers think about what kinds of questions to ask for what purposes, I also offer a heuristic to guide teachers in planning their questions and prompts, based on the skills they deem important and the challenges they are concerned about. This guide is depicted in Figure 2.2. Although this heuristic does not represent the full range of questions or issues that a teacher could explore in a think-aloud writing assessment session, it hopefully will give teachers a sense of where to start and inspiration to generate their own ideas.

I also want to include an important caveat about these planning tools: Their purpose is to provide a set of options for interacting with students in the think-aloud assessment, rather than a rigid script. I find Keith Sawyer's (2004) notion of "disciplined improvisation" helpful here as a way to reconcile the tension between spontaneity and planning in effective teaching interactions. According to Sawyer, disciplined improvisation offers "a way to conceptualize creative teaching within curricular structures" (p. 16). The teachers I have worked with have varied considerably in the degree to which they adhere to their list of preplanned questions. In fact, I have seen the same teacher vary the questions he or she asks depending on the needs of the individual student. And even when teachers do hew closely to the planned questions, they always improvise follow-up questions in response to the ideas that students generate. The planning should not determine all of the questions teachers ask; rather, its purpose is to help teachers be intentional and deliberate about the questions they ask. As I discussed in Chapter 1, good formative assessment practice is aligned with clear learning goals. Planning questions in advance, after careful review of an assigned writing task, is a good way to bring goals to the foreground and ensure that these goals will drive any questions asked in the think-aloud assessment, whether they are planned or spontaneous. Also, teachers should not expect to be able to anticipate all opportunities that might arise, but by engaging in some advance anticipation, they can prepare themselves to be responsive to the opportunities that do arise.

The conversational nature of interactive think-aloud writing assessment has many advantages, but there is at least one risk: that the interactions may become too informal and that teachers may lose sight of their goals or limit themselves to repeating the same kinds of questions or supports. For this

Figure 2.1. Template for specifying skills, challenges, and related questions for interactive think-aloud writing assessment

Skills that students need to be able to demonstrate with this writing task:	Questions I could ask to determine whether students have these skills:
1.	1.
2.	2.
3.	3.
4.	4.
5.	5.
6.	6.
Challenges that I anticipate my students might have in demonstrating these skills:	Questions I could ask to determine whether students are having these challenges:
1.	1.
2.	2.
3.	3.
4.	4.
5.	5.
6.	6.

reason, in addition to planning questions in advance, it may be helpful to consider the range of possible interactional moves that teachers and students can make in the interactive think-aloud assessment. Appendix B provides two typologies for this purpose: The first describes a set of moves that teachers can use to assess and support student writers, while the second describes student moves as responses to that support. The labels for the moves defined in these typologies are derived from studies of dynamic assessment with language learners (Poehner, 2008) and college-level writers (Shrestha & Coffin, 2012), along with my own analysis of the moves used by teachers and students I have worked with. These typologies may help teachers consider their own options for initiating support, to understand the bids that students make for support during think-aloud assessment sessions, and respond to those bids in optimally helpful ways.

Figure 2.2. Heuristic for planning interactive think-aloud writing assessment questions

If I want to know . . .	I could ask/say . . .
Task-specific skills and knowledge	
Whether students understand what the task is asking of them	In your own words, tell me what the prompt is asking you to do.
Whether the student understands how writing in this genre should be structured	How are you planning to organize this piece of writing?
Whether the student understands concepts that are essential to this writing task	Tell me in your own words what __ [concept] ___ means, and find an example of that for me [from the text or from general knowledge].
Whether students are aware of all resources available to help them complete the task	What are all the resources you could use to help you with this task? Which ones have you used? If you haven't used them all, why not?
Whether students are able to choose excerpts from text that support their thesis [relating to an argument about literature]	Show me the evidence you have chosen and explain to me how this supports your thesis.
Whether the student understands reader expectations for this type of writing	"So what?" Why are you telling us [readers] that? What am I supposed to understand from what you have just said/written?
General writing skills and knowledge	
Whether students are able to take up peer or teacher feedback and use it productively	What problems did you identify after peer editing, and how did you fix them?
Whether students can imagine the perspective of a reader on their own work	Read over this section and tell me if you've provided readers with everything they need to know in order to understand your point here.
What range of academic or discipline-specific language is available to the student	Can you think of a more literary [or "scientific" or "historical"] way to say that?
What the range of students' vocabulary is, generally	Is there a word you can use that is more vivid or nuanced?

Figure 2.2. Heuristic for planning interactive think-aloud writing assessment questions (continued)

If I want to know . . .	I could ask/say . . .
General writing skills and knowledge	
What the depth and range of students' grammatical knowledge is	Is that a complete sentence? Why or why not? You have a lot of short sentences that sound the same here. How could you change them to add variety?
Whether the student understands the difference between summary and analysis	What is analysis? Show me where you are doing that in the text you have written, or in what you just said.

Figure 2.3. Dimensions of think-aloud writing assessment

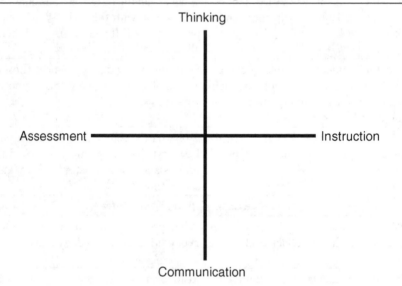

LINKING ASSESSMENT AND INSTRUCTION WITH THINK-ALOUD WRITING ASSESSMENT

A core principle of dynamic assessment is that assessment and instruction are intertwined. In adapting this principle for think-aloud writing assessment, I have found it helpful to think of this kind of assessment in terms of two axes that intersect at a 90-degree angle. On one axis is a continuum between assessment and instruction; on the other, a continuum between communication and thinking, as represented in Figure 2.3.

A teacher's dialogue with a student in an interactive assessment can take place in any of the four quadrants defined by these two axes. And over the course of the interaction, it can shift among quadrants. Let me illustrate this with the following example.

Ms. Miller has just sat down for a session with Diana about her essay on *Julius Caesar,* in which she responded to the prompt "Who should be the next leader of Rome now that Julius Caesar is dead?" with the choice of Brutus. The students have been working with a detailed set of scaffolds that includes examples of a thesis and topic sentences to introduce their body paragraphs, with space to write their own text following the models; a formula for introducing quotes (S.A.W. or Speaker, Audience, and What's Up?); and a mnemonic for constructing paragraphs known as TIEDIED, which stands for "**T**opic Sentence, **I**ntroduce **E**vidence, **E**vidence/Reason, **D**iscuss, **I**ntroduce **E**vidence, **E**vidence/Reason, **D**iscuss." Diana comes to the session having already written her introduction. Ms. Miller initiates the session with questions that reflect the upper left quadrant of Figure 2.3, assessing Diana's comprehension of the play by asking, "What are the two most important leadership traits of your candidate?" and continues this line of assessment-focused questions as follows:

1. *Diana:* That he's honorable and clever?
2. *Ms. Miller:* How does that connect to the values of Roman society?
3. *Diana:* So, being honorable and clever connects to having the Roman values because Romans value having honor. And then I feel if you're clever, then you kind of have some sort of sense of power, because you're able to manipulate the situation or make something happen as you want it to. And, power is also something that Romans value very much.
4. *Ms. Miller:* So who's the leader?
5. *Diana:* Brutus.
6. *Ms. Miller:* Okay. So, in what ways do you think he's clever?
7. *Diana:* I think he's clever because he appeals to the emotions of the crowd by justifying Caesar's death, like in the third act?
8. *Ms. Miller:* Mhm.
9. *Diana:* That whole speech when everyone was like: "Oh my god, how could he have died?" Caesar says, like he died—
10. *Ms. Miller:* Caesar or Brutus?
11. *Diana:* Brutus. He justifies [Caesar's] death by saying [pause of 10 seconds] that like, even though he died, there could always be a new leader because even though he was one of the best, he [Brutus] was pointing out all of his flaws. And so he was pointing out his [Caesar's] flaws, kind of making people say, "He was an okay leader, but not as good as we all thought 'cause he was doing this, this, and this wrong."

All of Ms. Miller' questions, in the interaction above are concerned with assessing what Diana understands about Brutus's character and the way that his character reflects Roman values. Assured that Diana's understanding of Brutus's rhetorical strategy is accurate, Ms. Miller shifts to the assessment of communication (the lower left quadrant of Figure 2.3), questioning Diana about how she can make her essay more cohesive—cohesion being an import-ant criterion for an effective essay—by relating her interpretation of Brutus's character to the quotes she has chosen. Ms. Miller's focus is now less on Diana's understanding of the character and more on how she plans to communicate that understanding in her essay:

> 12. *Ms. Miller:* Okay, good. So when you're using your quotes, how can you connect what you just said into those quotes? So, discussing that he's clever. 'Cause you said that you were struggling a little bit with this part. How can you make that connection into your quotes, and connect it back to your thesis statement?

This question prompts Diana to describe her plan for introducing the quotation, which reveals a misconception about the way the assignment re-quires her to introduce evidence:

> 13. *Diana:* Should I start off by saying that? I mean, I can say: "Brutus is the only one who can take Caesar's place," and then I can start by describing what was going on. So, "when the people of Rome were like nervous after they found out about Caesar's death, Brutus decides to make a speech to the people, expressing that . . ." Oh, no. I can say that "he decided to make a speech to the people in which he says . . ." and then make the quote . . .

Noticing that Diana is focusing not on analysis—that is, connecting her quotes to the thesis—but on the introduction of quotes (the "I" part of the TIEDIED structure), and that she is not following the formula, Ms. Miller makes two shifts in quick succession, first to the lower right quadrant of the diagram, instruction of communication, using this opportunity to re-teach the TIEDIED formula and remind Diana of what the requirements are for intro-ducing quotes:

> 14. *Ms. Miller:* So, can I make a suggestion? That would be your introduction to evidence, your "I" part. So, within that "I" part, I like the way that you say that you're gonna introduce it where you say like he's giving a speech and he, discusses, like, Caesar's traits of a leader and things like that. But it needs to be your "who, what, where, when, and why," right?

She then shifts back to assessment of communication, the lower left quad-rant of the diagram, asking Diana to evaluate what is missing in that introduc-tory section:

15. *Ms. Miller:* So it seems like you're missing part of it, right? So what do you think that you're missing? You don't just want to say, "and this is what he said," right? So what do you think you're missing in there?

Ms. Miller's question prompts Diana to review what she has written and fill in the missing information to Ms. Miller's satisfaction, checking her plans against the "who, what, where, when, why" heuristic, with Ms. Miller looking on. This interaction leads Diana to reveal that she still has some confusion over what goes into the introduction of evidence versus what goes into the discussion of evidence. This confusion was fairly common for Ms. Miller's students, who often, according to the team of three teachers who co-taught the humanities class, wrote strong analysis in the introductory sections of their paragraphs. Ms. Miller takes advantage of this interactional opportunity to address this confusion by shifting tactics again, this time combining assessment and instruction of communication. She assesses Diana's understanding of the purpose of the discussion section of the paragraph (in turn 26) and includes some additional explanatory instruction (in turn 32):

26. *Ms. Miller:* The discussion part is different because in the discussion part, you're doing what?
27. *Diana:* I'm like explaining the quote. . . . I'm explaining the evidence, like discussing it, right?
28. *Ms. Miller:* Okay, you're discussing it, and you're connecting it back to what?
29. *Diana:* To your thesis.
30. *Ms. Miller:* To your thesis, right? You don't want to give a summary in your discussion.
31. *Diana:* Okay.
32. *Ms. Miller:* So the discussion part should be where you're explaining why it's important, how it connects back to the values, what traits it's showing.

The series of moves described above culminates in Diana's fluent expression of new ideas for her discussion of evidence, in turns 33 and 35, which Ms. Miller enthusiastically approves:

33. *Diana:* He's pointing out all of Caesar's flaws . . .
34. *Ms. Miller:* Yep.
35. *Diana:* To make people think of him in a different way. And I can say, "This gives him a sense of power because he's kind of manipulating the way that the Romans are thinking, and power is a value that the Romans value."
36. *Ms. Miller:* Yeah! . . . Yeah! [laughing] That's good! Do you see how that's different from the introduction to evidence?

Through a strategic combination of questions and prompts that interweave assessment and instruction, Ms. Miller both identifies gaps in Diana's understanding of the task and of the text she is writing about, and guides her in repairing those gaps. The result, for the student, is both a more accurate understanding of Brutus's rhetorical tactics and a more coherent essay.

The interaction between Ms. Miller and Diana shows how dialogic, responsive instruction can occur at the level of essay organization, but it also can occur more locally at the level of the sentence and phrase. In the following excerpt from a think-aloud session between Ms. Stanley and Laura for an essay about *Pygmalion*, we see evidence of movement back and forth between assessment and instruction. Ms. Stanley intervenes in Laura's verbalizing of an idea for a sentence, with two sequential questions (turns 4 and 6) to assess her thinking. The first question flags Laura's interpretive phrase, "socialist attitude conjoined with language," as unclear:

1. *Laura:* So, what I wanna say now is that he uses a socialist attitude conjoined with language to show the problems of women and class.
2. *Ms. Stanley:* Just write it.
3. *Laura:* Okay.
4. *Ms. Stanley:* And by language what do you mean? "Socialist attitude conjoined with," what do you mean by language?
5. *Laura:* Like in the book, language is the most important thing, the fact that Eliza, she wasn't a part of the same class so she didn't kind of speak the same language, I think.
6. *Ms. Stanley:* So what is language, then?
7. *Laura:* Is it the social barrier?
8. *Ms. Stanley:* Sure, yeah, okay. Conjoins.
9. *Laura:* [writing] Conjoins language . . .
10. *Ms. Stanley:* Mm-hmm. I mean you could just put, "as a social barrier," right?
11. *Laura:* Oh, okay, right. I don't like the sentence.
12. [Laughter]
13. *Laura:* I'm sorry.
14. *Ms. Stanley:* That's okay.
15. *Laura:* Because this is how I really write.
16. *Ms. Stanley:* Yeah.

Ms. Stanley's question in turn 4 prompts the student to verbalize her understanding of the significance of language in the representation of Eliza Doolittle. Not content to merely accept this example, Ms. Stanley presses again for a definition ("so what is language, then?" in turn 6). By asking a question that appears to be assessing the student's understanding of important concepts in the play, Ms. Stanley prompts the student to recognize that she is not saying what she wants to say. Then Ms. Stanley supports her in correcting this problem by providing direct instruction in communication in turn 10, suggesting a particular sentence formulation. In the writing that she completed during this think-aloud assessment session, Laura revised the sentence "Shaw effectively conveys a socialist attitude that conjoins language with social class," and replaced it with the more explicit formulation "Shaw effectively conveys a socialist attitude that depicts language as the social barrier of class"—more explicit in that it introduces the notion of "barrier." Revising one sentence to include a more precise formulation of her idea allowed her to elaborate on her ideas with two other aspects of Shaw's socialist attitude. This is the sentence that she ultimately settled on during this session: *Shaw effectively conveys a socialist attitude that depicts language as the social barrier of class, a predestined gender dynamic, and a wealth-based social hierarchy.*

Of course, thinking and communication are interdependent; there is not such a clear boundary between them as Figure 2.3 would suggest. Yet, this diagram may help remind teachers of these two facets of academic writing, and guide teachers in planning how to navigate between them. Teachers should not think that they have to focus on *either* assessment *or* teaching, but should be aware of which intention they are foregrounding at any moment in the interaction. Teachers also should consider that any one move may serve multiple purposes. For example, providing instruction to help students overcome communicative challenges also can help them overcome obstacles in their thinking. An example of this kind of effect can be seen in Mr. Tancredi's work with Elisa. Elisa is working on an analysis of "The Rime of the Ancient Mariner" and is having trouble understanding the meaning of the phrase "life in death." She has just written the assertion that "life in death wasn't a good place to be," and Mr. Tancredi asks, assessing her understanding, "Why isn't it a good place to be?"

> *Elisa:* Because it's not really an ending. It's not a life or death. It's like eternal life in death. So, you're kind of like in a daydream basically. And it's not reality or it's not death. It's just—I don't know what it is.
> *Mr. Tancredi:* Let's try to capture that idea in writing. Right? How would you start explaining that concept? Maybe a catch word to redirect the reader.
> *Elisa:* Lucid? Mmm, not lucid.

Having assessed that Elisa is still struggling, Mr. Tancredi pivots to an instructional move:

> *Mr. Tancredi:* Have you ever watched *The Golden Girls*? [Elisa nods] So, when the little old lady is about to tell a story, what does she say? "Picture it. Imagine it." So, she's prompting. The audience knows she's about to go on a little tangent, right? So, how about you use something like that right here?

This suggestion prompts a spurt of composing from Elisa, in which she produces the sentence, "Think about it as if you weren't living and you weren't dead, but you were living in eternal death." This is a new formulation of the idea, one that implies a deeper level of understanding and satisfies both her and Mr. Tancredi. This example shows the interdependence of thinking and communicating in writing, and how supporting one, as Mr. Tancredi did with the rhetorical strategy borrowed from a familiar TV show, can support the other.

Teachers will want to keep in mind that whether a particular move constitutes assessment or instruction can depend on how students respond to that move. As an illustration of this distinction, let's look at how a student responds to Mr. Almador's use of the "reflecting and recalling" move, which refers to when a teacher "says back" what a student has just said, or reminds the student of something said previously. One effect of using this move is to provide instructional support, in that the teacher functions as a kind of external working memory for the student, providing an interactional cognitive scaffold. But this move also elicits assessment information, as we can see in the excerpt below between Mr. Almador and his student, Leila, who is beginning to draft her essay about *The Great Gatsby*. Mr. Almador begins by reminding the student of an interpretive statement she had made several turns earlier and asks her to clarify that statement:

> *Mr. Almador:* I want to backtrack a little bit. You had said something that you feel that Fitzgerald is trying to say that women all want something different. Like, they all have different ideals for what they want out of life. But, I'm just wondering, when you say that, isn't that true of, just, men and women? Right? Don't men and women want something different out of life? Isn't that just an individual?

His "reflecting" strategy, coupled with a request for elaboration, functions instructionally to draw the student out and prompt deeper reflection on the reading in the following turns, which Mr. Almador responds to by offering encouraging "Mhmms."

> *Leila:* I guess, like, what he could be trying to say is that usually, like, one has an ideal, like, that a woman wants to be married kind of like for a sense of security. Like, you know, you think of a woman and you don't really think they're independent, I guess, in that time. You think that, you know, the dream, like you said, is to get married and have a home and everything like that. So, he's trying to show how, you know, each of them, in a way, like, has a different social class. Like, you know Myrtle?
> *Mr. Almador:* Mhmm.
> *Leila:* Like, I told you, she wants the wealth. But then Daisy's already up there.

Mr. Almador: Mhmm.

Leila: So, then maybe Daisy, like I'll really contrast her with Jordan.

Mr. Almador: Okay.

Leila: Because Jordan is like Daisy. She is wealthy. But then, unlike her, she's showing that she doesn't need to have a husband.

Mr. Almador: Mhmm.

A few turns later, though, Mr. Almador's repetition of the student's thesis elicits the student's self-assessment of some uncertainty:

Leila: But then Daisy, she could be independent, like if she's unhappy with Tom, she could leave, but there's obviously something stopping her from doing so. So, I think what he could be showing is that, no matter what, the social class is, like, for women, they don't need to maybe get married. They shouldn't rely on a man for that.

Mr. Almador: So you feel right now that that's, at least for now, your working thesis—what Fitzgerald is trying to say is that women do not need to rely on a man.

Leila: For now. Like it could possibly change as I, you know, compare them.

Mr. Almador: Okay.

Leila: But I feel like right now that's what I really have, and I don't know if it works or not.

Mr. Almador's "reflecting and recalling" move functions both as instruction and assessment in this interaction. At the beginning of this exchange it seems to function as part of an assessment move, in that he probes her thinking about Fitzgerald's views on the difference between men and women, but it also, instructionally, prompts her to clarify this thinking. When Mr. Almador restates her thesis, in the excerpt above, this restatement functions to assess whether he has understood the thesis correctly, and it also surfaces some uncertainty—assessing the student's thinking in two different ways. Although the teacher's strategy is the same in both cases, its ultimate function differs depending on how the student responds.

The shift between assessment and instruction often evolves organically in response to the teacher's perception of what the student needs and, because these shifts cannot be anticipated, they cannot be planned in advance. However, if teachers approach a think-aloud assessment session with a clear sense of the skills they have prioritized for the writing task, they will be primed to act on opportunities to shift from assessment to instruction and from a focus on thinking to a focus on communication. Later in this chapter, I give examples of planning tools that teachers can use to prepare themselves to make the most of these opportunities.

THINK-ALOUD WRITING ASSESSMENT VERSUS WRITING CONFERENCES

Working one-on-one with students to develop their writing through interactive think-aloud assessment is in some ways similar to the writing conference, an instructional practice with a long history and documentation in empirical research. Like writing conferences (Ewert, 2009; Patthey-Chavez & Ferris, 1997; Vygotsky, 1978; Weissberg, 2006), the interactive think-aloud assessment allows teachers to target feedback to learners' respective zones of proximal development and to socialize students into the language practices of particular disciplines (Duff, 2010). And, like writing conferences, think-aloud assessment may be useful at any point in the writing process—when the student is struggling to begin, when the student is midway through a draft, or when a draft has been completed and the student is about to undertake a revision. The essential difference between writing conferences as typically practiced and interactive think-aloud writing assessment is that the latter should be designed for the teacher to observe and support the process of composing—whether generating an initial draft or revising a completed draft—with focused, intentional questions and prompts, and for the student to "think aloud" as much as possible. This allows for more immediate identification of the challenges that writers experience and responses to those challenges.

An analogy to music lessons may be a helpful way to understand the difference between typical writing conferences and interactive think-aloud assessment; for this, I'll draw on my own experience studying guitar for the past 2 years. A conference that begins with a focus on something a student has already written, and where the talk is about what could be improved in the draft, would be akin to me presenting my guitar teacher with a video recording of myself playing, and asking for feedback and critique. In a video recording, he would likely notice mistakes and offer suggestions for improvement, and I would have to remember this feedback and try to apply it the next time I sat down to play. Instead, with real-time feedback during a lesson, the guitar teacher is doing what a writing teacher can do with think-aloud assessment: listening to and observing a student engaged in the process of doing the work, and providing immediate feedback that can be incorporated as part of that process, such as suggesting how to change finger position to get a better sound on the fretboard or demonstrating it himself.

PLANNING AND RECORD-KEEPING

Think-aloud assessment of writing should be organized around goals, so it's important for teachers to have a method for planning how they will interact with students and keep a record of what they learn.

The developers of dynamic assessment have made a distinction between *interactionist* and *interventionist* versions of this approach, which can be helpful for teachers to consider when they are planning an interactive think-aloud session. In an interventionist approach, the teacher uses the same prompts and questions with all students, with the aim of standardizing the supports and comparing how different types of students respond to the same support. This approach may be useful if, for example, a teacher is interested in using the interactive think-aloud method with a select group of students to discern whether certain heuristic tools or routine strategies might be useful to implement for the whole class. However, many teachers may find this too scripted. The advantage of the interactionist approach, by contrast, is that it enables the teacher to respond to students' unique needs as they become apparent in a think-aloud assessment session. For teachers who have never used think-aloud assessment before, it is likely that doing so will reveal strengths and challenges not previously considered; in this case, then the option to be more individually responsive is an advantage.

In order to compare how these two approaches would lead to different kinds of planning, I offer the comparison of two different sets of planning and record-keeping sheets, based on the same set of skills specified in Mr. Almador's classroom. He had given his student a choice of two assignments, one of which is reproduced here. The skills in Figure 2.4 and questions in Figures 2.5 and 2.6. are based on this assignment:

> Identify F. Scott Fitzgerald's view of the American dream as communicated in *The Great Gatsby*. Describe the tone and mood of the text and explain how the author uses archetypes and symbols to communicate its philosophical message. Provide clear and accurate examples and evidence from the text and analyze by using insightful commentary and criticism.

Mr. Almador—like all of the teachers I have worked with so far—used a more interactionist approach in working with students on an essay about *The Great Gatsby*. He came up with a set of questions he could ask to determine whether students had the skills he was interested in assessing (Figure 2.4). These questions are listed in Figure 2.5.

In the think-aloud assessment sessions, Mr. Almador did not ask all of these questions, and he asked some questions not listed here. He also did more than ask questions. For example, "reflecting and recalling student ideas" was a move he frequently employed. The approach he took was more interactionist than interventionist. However, a teacher could use questions like his in an interventionist way by making sure to ask all of them. Or, a teacher could make the questions more specific and build in some extra support for students who might need it. Figure 2.6 depicts a revised version of Mr. Almador's questions that illustrates a plan for more structured support.

This version of the questions includes more instructional support, such as the definition of terms included in questions 1, 6, 8, and 11. Asking whether students know these terms can help teachers understand whether a lack of understanding of their meaning is hindering students' writing. In a similar way, question 5 includes the option of providing a formula for students to use to

Figure 2.4. Skills that students needed to be able to demonstrate for Mr. Almador's essay on _The Great Gatsby_

1. Interpret the prompt accurately.
2. Write an easily identifiable thesis (argument that addresses a specific idea that the student will analyze and prove in the essay).
3. Write clear topic sentences that clearly connect to the thesis.
4. Organize paragraphs that convey a coherent argument.
5. Maintain the focus of argument so that the point of each paragraph is always clear.
6. Identify quotes that relate to the chosen subject (women in the novel or the American dream).
7. Make insightful inferences about the chosen subject.
8. Convincingly support all inferences with text-based evidence on the chosen subject.
9. Establish and maintain a formal style, using precise language and sound structure.
10. Demonstrate control of the conventions with infrequent errors.

Figure 2.5. Questions that Mr. Almador thought he could ask to assess whether a student had these skills

1. In your own words, what is the prompt asking you to do?
2. What is your plan for the essay?
3. Can a reader easily identify and understand what the writer is trying to analyze and prove in this essay?
4. How does your topic sentence connect to the main point you are trying to prove and/or analyze?
5. What is Fitzgerald's definition of the American dream?
6. What is the tone and mood that the story communicates?
7. How does the narrator convey the tone and mood?
8. What is an archetype?
9. What archetype does the main character represent?
10. What quotes support your assertion of which archetype the main character represents?
11. What is symbolism?
12. What ideas do the symbols represent?
13. How did you prove your thesis?

Figure 2.6. An interventionist revision of some of the questions in Figure 2.5

1. In your own words, what is the prompt asking you to do?

   a. To *identify* means to name in clear and understandable language.

   b. To *describe* means to use vivid and specific words, often adjectives, to make an event or idea understood by the reader.

   c. *Commentary* is your own original thoughts on what this evidence means in relation to Fitzgerald's view of the American dream.

   Thinking about these definitions, try stating in your own words what the prompt is asking you to do.

2. What is your plan for the essay?

   a. An essay has a beginning, middle, and end. What will you do in each section of the essay?

3. Can a reader easily identify and understand what the writer is trying to analyze and prove in this essay?

   a. Read what you have written back to me, and tell me if you think it would be understandable to a reader.

4. How does your topic sentence connect to the main point you are trying to prove and/or analyze?

5. What is Fitzgerald's definition of the American dream? If you are having trouble, use the formula below to fill in the blanks.

   a. F. Scott Fitzgerald believes that the American dream is [insert adjective] _____. He believes this because [insert statement/description of actions that illustrate adjective] _____.

6. What is tone? What is mood?

   a. *Tone* in literature is defined as the author's attitude toward the actions and ideas in a work.

   b. *Mood* in literature is the feeling that the setting, characters, and action create in the reader.

   What are the tone and mood that the story communicates?

7. How does the narrator convey the tone and mood?

8. What is an archetype?

   a. An archetype is a typical character with a pattern of behavior that other characters represent or enact.

9. What archetype does each main character represent?

10. What quotes show these typical patterns of behavior?

Figure 2.6. An interventionist revision of some of the questions in Figure 2.5 (continued)

11. What is symbolism?

    a. Symbolism is the use of objects or images to represent abstract ideas.

    b. What are some examples of symbolism in *The Great Gatsby*?

12. How will you prove your thesis about the American dream using . . .

    a. mood?

    b. tone?

    c. archetypes?

    d. symbols?

---

construct a thesis statement. Asking the questions first with less support—for example, "What is the prompt asking you to do?"—and then following up with more support if the student cannot provide a satisfactory answer, is a way for teachers to get a sense of the range of support that students in any given class need in order to successfully complete a writing task.

QUESTIONS TEACHERS MAY HAVE

1. How can I avoid talking too much, in order to make space for students to speak? How do I resist the impulse to fix the student's problems?

The default interactional patterns and instructional routines that prevail in classrooms lead teachers to expect to give answers and to be rewarded for doing so. It takes a shift in mindset to overcome these typical patterns, and one way to do this is to focus on making the students feel as if they have space to speak during the think-aloud assessment session. Here are some examples of how to start a session at any point in the writing process with an open-ended prompt:

> **Example 1** (at the very beginning)
> *Teacher:* In your own words, what was the prompt asking you to do?
> **Example 2** (in the middle)
> *Teacher:* You have a draft of your first paragraph here. What are you thinking about how you want to continue?
> **Example 3** (revision after first draft)
> *Teacher:* Which part needs the most work? Read through that part and tell me what you want to change.

Avoiding the temptation to answer students' questions can lead students to figure out a problem on their own, as in this exchange between Ms. Stanley and Ramona, in which Ramona toggles back and forth between the ideas that she has brainstormed and the requirements for the writing task about *Pygmalion*, which is:

> Why are there so many references to "what is to become" of Eliza? What broader concern for society might Shaw be expressing? In other words, consider which characters are raising these concerns, the conflicts these concerns represent in relation to Eliza and society, and how Shaw might be resolving these conflicts.

The student rereads, "consider which characters are raising these concerns, the conflicts these concerns represent in relation to Eliza and society, how Shaw might be resolving these conflicts," and asks, "So, is it in a way compare and contrast?" Rather than answer this question directly, Ms. Stanley prompts her to "keep talking," and the exchange proceeds as follows:

1. *Ramona:* Like Mr. Doolittle.
2. *Ms. Stanley:* Okay.
3. *Ramona:* [writing] Mr. Doolittle because he also kind of reflects Eliza, but almost in a satirical way, and he's more up-front.
4. *Ms. Stanley:* Does he link to anything you said here? 'Cause this is really good. So don't lose what you have—it's really good. Does he link to any of these statements that you have?
5. *Ramona:* The morals.
6. *Ms. Stanley:* Yeah.
7. *Ramona:* He doesn't have morals.
8. *Ms. Stanley:* And why? Do you remember what he said? Can't afford them.
9. *Ramona:* Oh, 'cause he calls them "middle-class morals."
10. *Ms. Stanley:* Yeah.
11. *Ramona:* And I guess, like, the more money you have, it's easier. Like, when you reference donating money to a widow.
12. *Ms. Stanley:* Mmmhmm.

Rather than answer her questions, Ms. Stanley encourages the student to keep talking, gives affirmation (turns 6, 10, and 12), asks questions to further probe her thinking (turn 4), and provides a clue from the text that steers the student toward the theme of money (turn 8, "Can't afford them."). By restraining any impulse to solve the student's problems, Ms. Stanley gives the student time and space to get closer to her thesis, which turns out to be "social class does not stem from a name or wealth but from character and knowledge."

A good general rule for teachers to follow is to try not to answer a student's question until they (a) feel they have fully understood what the problem is, and (b) are sure the student cannot figure out the answer on his or her own. Teachers should try providing hints first, before giving the student a complete answer or solution. Keeping track of when students can resolve a problem with a hint can give a teacher a sense of what might work as helpful scaffolding for other students in the class.

2. When should I intervene with a solution? How much intervention is too much?

Waiting for a student to arrive at an answer on his or her own is often not logistically possible, because of time constraints, or morally desirable, because we don't want to make students uncomfortable by subjecting them to protracted cognitive—and often emotional—struggles in front of a witness, their teacher. When teacher questioning reveals that a student's composing process is blocked by a misconception or gap in knowledge, it can be productive to intervene by correcting the misconception, filling the gap, or providing instructional support to help the student overcome the challenge. Mr. Tancredi's reference to the "picture this" rhetorical strategy borrowed from a TV show in his interaction with Elisa is one example of such intervention. Another is Ms. Miller's re-teaching of the TIEDIED organizational structure with Diana.

3. How should I follow up with students after a think-aloud assessment session?

One type of follow-up is instructional feedback, which is a key characteristic of any assessment that is used formatively (Cizek, 2010; Erickson, 2007; Heritage, 2010; Shepard, 2000; Wiliam, 2010). As I've shown in some of the examples above, feedback is built into the interactive version of think-aloud writing assessment. But on a longer time-scale, follow-up entails giving students a sense of where they need to go next and checking in to determine whether they have gotten to that objective. Frequently, the teachers I have worked with conclude their sessions with guidance on what they want students to work on next, with statements and interactions such as the following:

> *Mr. Almador:* Okay, all right, so that's what we need to do, either find a connection, or if it doesn't work we might need to look for another symbol to help you. But that was awesome, both the archetype and mood. That was very insightful, especially what you said about mood, right, so you do what you did with this with a symbol, try to relate it back to your thesis statement.
> Or:
> *Mr. Tancredi:* Tomorrow is our last day working on this. Tonight I definitely want you to think about that conclusion.
> *Alex:* I have a lot of things I can compare it to. It's just to pick the ones that
> . . .
> *Mr. Tancredi:* Correct. And you've got to keep your details to a minimum. If you keep adding and adding and adding details—

Alex: Adding and adding, it'll prolong the time.
Mr. Tancredi: —you'll prolong the time you needed to write.

Having set goals for students' next steps in the work, teachers can check in with students quickly on the next day to see whether they've met those goals, or, if the goals are observable within the texts (e.g., "keep details to a minimum," above), they can assess whether students have met the goals by analyzing their written drafts.

4. Practically speaking, how do I implement this type of individualized assessment when I am responsible for as many as 120 students?

Given the individualized and time-intensive nature of this type of assessment, it may not be possible to conduct this assessment with all students in each marking period. It's important to keep in mind that think-aloud writing assessment is a *qualitative* assessment and is not designed or intended to be used for the purpose of grading or scoring. This should alleviate some of the pressure to attempt to conduct this assessment with all students during a marking period. An important consideration to keep in mind is that think-aloud writing assessment sessions need not be long to be effective. Focusing on one or two aspects of a writing task, or one or two writing skills, and exploring those in depth will be more useful and effective than trying to check many boxes in one session. Some of the teachers I have worked with have had success in conducting think-aloud assessment sessions in one corner of the room while the rest of the class works independently. The recommendations I offered for selecting students in Chapter 1 are important to reiterate and elaborate on here: (1) Students should be comfortable verbalizing their thoughts in front of a partner, and while ideally the teacher will have created a classroom environment where this is the case for most if not all students, it may take longer for some students to reach that level of comfort than others; and (2) think-aloud assessment may be most revealing, at least at first, when used with students whose writing has not progressed in response to typical instruction. Teachers I have worked with have used words like *puzzle* and *mystery* to describe the students with whom they want to work in think-aloud assessment.

5. Can students work with peers in think-aloud assessment?

One way of addressing the time commitment involved in think-aloud assessment, as in any individualized type of assessment, is to develop the capacity of students to serve as peer assessors for one another. There is good reason to believe that peer support through think-aloud assessment can be as effective as teacher support, if not more so. Peer response to writing is valuable for several reasons: (1) it makes student writers aware of the influence of audience considerations in the writing process; (2) it provides an authentic context for communication—more authentic in some ways than writing for a teacher; (3) it helps writers develop genre knowledge; and (4) it helps student writers develop a "meta-language" for writing—that is, language they can use to talk about and reflect on their choices as writers (Hoogveen & van Gelderen, 2013). Researchers have been studying peer response in writing for several decades now, and we know from this research that routines for writing instruction that incorporate peer response are among the most effective types of interventions, second only to teacher-led strategy instruction and instruction in summarizing source text (Graham & Perin, 2007). When it comes to evaluating students' writing, the average of multiple students' ratings of an essay is often closer than a teacher's rating to expert ratings of the same essay (Schunn, Godley, & DiMartino, 2016). These findings, taken together, give us good reason to believe that peers can be a powerful resource for assessment and teaching of writing through think-aloud assessment.

However, guidance and training are necessary to harness and channel this power. Based on my interpretation of the literature on effective peer response to writing, and peer-assisted learning more generally (helpfully summarized in *Effective Peer Learning: From Principles to Practical Implementation* [Topping, Buchs, Duran, & van Keer, 2017]), I suggest that teachers use the following principles as guidance in setting up a peer-assisted model of think-aloud writing assessment:

1. *Take time to model and practice effective interaction in a think-aloud session.* Because writing is a complex process, think-aloud assessment of peers' writing process is also more complex than, for example, a checklist for review of an essay draft. We know that the more complex a peer-assisted activity is, the more important it is to train students systematically in how to manage the interactions in peer-assisted learning (Topping et al., 2017). The teacher might consider training a small group of students by conducting interactive think-alouds with them first, then inviting them to assist in modeling sessions for the whole class. This core group of students can then be the first to engage in interactive think-alouds with other peers, in a peer-training model.

2. *Collaboratively generate a framework for the skills to be assessed and moves for peer tutors to use.* Peer-assisted think-aloud assessment is another way to help students feel like stakeholders in the assessment of writing. Teachers can work with the whole class to do the skills identification and question planning for the interactive think-aloud.

3. *Strategically prioritize genre-specific aspects of writing for peers to focus on.* Research on peer response to writing has suggested that instruction in specific genre knowledge—defined as the types of vocabulary and grammatical structures used to create genres—makes peer response sessions more effective than does giving students only general guidelines about effective communication (such as "make sure your writing is

clear" or "make sure you explain your evidence") (Hoogeveen & van Gelderen, 2015). The teacher move labeled "metalinguistic clues" (see Appendix B) can be especially useful for this purpose.

4. *Make it routine.* As with any complex skill, it takes time to become adept in think-aloud assessment, and regular practice helps students become proficient as well as comfortable with the process. Teachers may want to require that students use certain moves or ask certain questions at first, but as students become more practiced in peer-assisted think-aloud assessment, they can be gradually released from these requirements.

CONCLUSION

My aim in this chapter has been to describe how adding interaction to think-aloud writing assessment can realize the full dialogic potential of this approach, and to give teachers some principles and tactics for doing so. By engaging in a dialogic interaction with students as they verbalize their writing processes, the teacher allows students to become more aware of the audience for their writing and can reveal the skills that emerge in the student's zone of proximal development for writing. I have laid out several parameters for teachers to consider as they plan their interactive work with students: Will they be assessing, instructing, or both? Will they focus more on thinking or more on communicating, or give equal attention to both? And, how much do they want to be able to compare what they learn from these individualized assessments across students, and how much do they want to customize the assessment for each learner? These parameters offer teachers much to consider as they embark on this new approach to understanding the composing processes of developing adolescent writers.

CHAPTER 3

What Can Teachers Learn from Think-Aloud Writing Assessment?

A FOCUS ON INDIVIDUAL STUDENT NEEDS

Decades of research on writing instruction have led to the conclusion that using assessment data to inform writing instruction is a key element of an effective schoolwide writing program (Graham & Perin, 2007). This is consistent with findings from an often-cited review on the impact of formative assessment generally, which showed that its use raises achievement for all learners, but especially those learners most vulnerable to failure (Black & Wiliam, 1998). One possible reason for this effect is that formative assessment requires teachers to pay close attention to individual learners' needs, using the information they obtain from assessments to inform their instruction. As I'll discuss in Chapter 5, student learning also plays a key role in formative assessment; indeed, according to many assessment scholars, student participation is the defining characteristic of formative assessment. However, in this chapter, my focus is on what teachers can learn about students from think-aloud writing assessment.

Much of the research that has examined teacher learning from formative assessment has focused on teachers looking together at interim or benchmark assessment data in school-level teams. Interim or benchmark assessments are those designed to monitor progress toward curricular objectives. Though this is an important purpose of assessments, it tends to be difficult for teachers to interpret the information they obtain from these assessments in ways that are helpful for planning instruction (Shepard, 2005), because these assessments are designed to produce information that is easy to aggregate at the school or class level, and not to be used to address individual student needs (Datnow & Hubbard, 2015).

To explore student learning in more depth, we need assessment methods that allow us to see students as individuals. This was the motivation of Shannon Pella's (2012) study of a small group of middle school ELA teachers who turned their backs on their school's exclusive reliance on benchmark tests as a focus of teacher professional development in favor of what's known as a "lesson-study" (Lewis, Perry, & Murata, 2006) approach that involved close qualitative analysis of students' writing and observations of one another's writing instruction. This approach led the teachers to develop instruction that was more responsive to students' challenges. Assessment scholars in subjects other than ELA have made claims about the value of classroom-based qualitative and individualized assessment for promoting student learning. For example, Ruiz-Primo (2011) has proposed that what she calls "assessment conversations" integrated within science classroom activities can be an effective way of allowing teachers to discern students' misconceptions and adjust their teaching accordingly, thereby leading to measurably better learning outcomes for students.

The assessment tool probably employed most commonly to support teachers' close qualitative evaluation of student writing is the rubric, a tool that indeed has many affordances. Rubrics can help teachers provide more precise and constructive feedback (Allen, Ort, & Schmidt, 2009; Fry & Griffin, 2010) while also helping students develop the capacity to think metacognitively about their writing (Andrade, Wang, Du, & Akawi, 2009). At the same time, however, rubrics can narrow teachers' conceptions of good writing and prevent them from recognizing students' unique goals, talents, and achievements as writers (Spence, 2010; Wilson, 2007). This is a meaningful limitation, insofar as assessment for learning is supposed to focus on student strengths (Stiggins, 2001). Rubrics also don't take students' writing process into account, or allow teachers to give feedback on students' use of writing strategies. This limitation may hamper teachers' ability to implement the kind of strategy-based instruction that we know to be especially effective in supporting developing writers (de la Paz & Graham, 2002).

LEARNING ABOUT STUDENTS' WRITING PROCESSES

Colleagues and I (Beck et al., 2015) worked with a group of teachers who used think-aloud writing assessment without any questions or prompting. We compared the inferences that teachers made about students' writing when they listened to and observed students thinking aloud while composing, with the inferences they made based on their typical, product-based approaches to writing assessment—for example, grading papers based on a rubric. Not surprisingly, we found that the think-aloud as an assessment tool gave teachers insights about writing process that they hadn't noticed at all when looking only at students' writing. More specifically, we found that listening to students think aloud enabled teachers to make inferences about students' ability to evaluate, to focus, to recall important information from the book they were writing about, and to manage their own writing processes. None of these aspects of writing surfaced when teachers assessed students without using the think-aloud approach. As shown in the examples that I discuss below, these new insights also led teachers to make adjustments to their feedback to students and, in some cases, to their follow-up instruction.

Evaluating

Being able to evaluate one's own writing accurately and to self-regulate are characteristics of a proficient writer. Observing whether and how effectively students evaluate their own work as they think aloud can help teachers correct mistaken assumptions about what students may, or may not, be doing as they write. This is useful information because the instructional follow-up—teaching them that they need to evaluate their writing, teaching them how to evaluate their writing, and remedying ineffective strategies for evaluating writing—would be applied differently depending on what the teacher learns from listening to students think aloud while writing. For example, Mr. Binder noticed that when Greg, whose papers typically were littered with typos and small grammatical errors, reread his own writing aloud, he automatically corrected the errors. Merely telling students like Greg to "reread your work" would not be sufficient to address this problem. Evaluating is an important part of the writing process for students, not only for fixing grammatical and mechanical errors, but also for evaluating the quality of the content they are generating or how clearly they are expressing their ideas. For example, the think-aloud assessment has been helpful in revealing the processes that result in incoherent writing—whether due to students not taking the time to evaluate ideas that come to mind very quickly, or whether they do in fact evaluate their ideas but then have trouble figuring out how to put them in order or how to render, in the grammar of written language, the transitions among ideas. Looking at students' writing alone can offer only a partial picture of the nature of students' struggles with writing, whereas think-aloud assessment enables teachers to understand students' writing process more fully and adjust their pedagogy accordingly.

Being able to make observations about the extent to which students evaluate their work also can illuminate what students are doing well in this regard. For example, Ms. Lindner observed that Barbara's tactic of "looking back and changing things and having an awareness of what didn't make sense" was consistent with the "polished" quality of her finished work. For Ms. Lindner, listening to think-alouds also revealed the degree of effort that went into polished writing. For instance, she was surprised by Janet's habit of stopping and thinking while trying to spell certain words. As Ms. Lindner pointed out, when you see something done correctly in a finished draft, you have no way of knowing how much effort or how many attempts went into producing that correct version.

When planning for think-aloud assessment by designing a record sheet or planning questions to ask in an interactive think-aloud session, teachers should keep in mind the unique opportunity to assess processes, including strategies and decisionmaking, and should resist focusing on skills and knowledge that could be assessed by analyzing students' writing with a rubric. This means that text-focused concerns such as "clear thesis" and "coherent argument" are best reframed as "synthesize interpretation of the poem into a clear thesis about the role of the supernatural," or "perceive and articulate links between textual evidence chosen and the central claim or thesis." Teachers also can learn much from focusing on skills that are not specific to any one writing task or written genre. For example, Mr. Tancredi specified "time management" as an important skill, while Ms. Schnader specified "identify challenges from peer editing and make appropriate corrections" as one of the skills she deemed necessary to complete the writing assignment (an essay on *Othello*). Because Ms. Schnader probed for students' reasoning about the changes they made during the think-aloud sessions, as illustrated in the following interaction with Leslie, she was able to determine that Leslie was able to self-assess and self-correct, and that an appropriate next step would be to give her more complex writing tasks:

> *Leslie:* In . . . the . . . book . . . Othello . . . Iago . . . was . . . telling . . . was . . . Iago was . . . informing . . .
> *Ms. Schnader:* Hmm, why did you change it to *informing*?
> *Leslie:* Because it sounds better to me.
> (And several turns later):
> *Leslie:* So . . . when . . . Othello . . . found . . . out . . . he . . . couldn't . . . believe . . . it. I'm going to make this into two sentences.
> *Ms. Schnader:* Hmm, how come?
> *Leslie:* Because it's an add-on.
> *Ms. Schnader:* Okay.
> *Leslie:* I mean a run-on.
> *Ms. Schnader:* That's okay, I understood.

These interactions led Ms. Schnader to conclude that Leslie was capable of self-assessing and revising her own writing in an autonomous way, and that the logical next step for her would be to attempt more complicated writing tasks. Ms. Schnader also determined that she should break out of the rigid critical lens essay formula that she had been teaching the students for most of the year, as required by her school's administration.

Ms. Schnader reached a somewhat different conclusion when she worked with another student, Dorinda. As with Leslie, she probed during the think-aloud session to explore Dorinda's assessment of her own work. She began by asking Dorinda to read her introductory paragraph out loud, then asked questions such as "Does that set you up to answer the prompt?" and "What doesn't make sense?" after Dorinda admitted that she thought her analysis didn't make sense. Dorinda responded to the latter question by rereading a sentence fragment from her text: "But it says "which led him to commit a gruesome act," then adds, "I think I should explain that more." The following exchange ensued:

> *Ms. Schnader:* Okay, okay, sounds good. Is that a full sentence?
> *Dorinda:* No, it's not.

Ms. Schnader: Okay, how could you make that a full sentence?

Dorinda: It's a fragment. I could say, which led him to commit a gruesome act. Um, which led him to, which led him to kill his wife. How about that?

Ms. Schnader: Okay, yeah. Making it more specific.

At the beginning of this think-aloud session, Dorinda determines that her writing "doesn't make sense," but is not able to independently correct the problem she has identified. To support Dorinda in moving from identifying the problem to correcting it, Ms. Schnader tries to focus the student's attention on the grammatical status of the statement "which led him to commit a gruesome act" by asking: "Is that a full sentence?" This effort does not lead to a grammatical correction but rather a rephrasing of the action in more precise language ("kill his wife" rather than "a gruesome act"), which Ms. Schnader accepts as an improvement. This revision is then followed by a productive bout of composing in which Dorinda generates a new interpretive idea:

1. *Dorinda:* Instead of saying a gruesome act, because I don't really know what I'm talking about. Okay. [*types*] And I can say this shows . . . how jealousy... is a hatred built upon insecurity? It still doesn't make sense, does it now, right?
2. *Ms. Schnader:* What doesn't make sense?
3. *Dorinda:* I said, this shows how jealousy is a hatred built upon insecurity?
4. *Ms. Schnader:* Okay, yeah, what does that mean?
5. *Dorinda:* Jealousy is like, built on insecurity, so like somebody tell you something, you're gonna believe it, and gonna build on, and then that's why you gonna envy someone, 'cause they're doing, 'cause like they are what you wanna be.
6. *Ms. Schnader:* Okay, is a hatred built up on insecurity, so add what you just said right there.
7. *Dorinda:* What? I don't even know what . . . uh . . . built upon insecurities . . .
8. *Ms. Schnader:* Okay, so say it out loud as you do it. What are you thinking?
9. *Dorinda:* This shows how jealousy is a hatred built upon insecurities, meaning . . .
10. *Ms. Schnader:* Okay, good.
11. *Dorinda:* Hatred . . . I mean, meaning low self-esteem can lead you to envy others who are the ideal . . .
12. *Ms. Schnader:* Oooh!
13. *Dorinda:* . . . version that you want to be? Or ideal?
14. *Ms. Schnader:* Oooh! That sounds really deep.

In turn 1 above, Dorinda voices dissatisfaction with the clarity of the statement that jealousy is "hatred built upon insecurity." To support her in making a revision, Ms. Schnader asks her to explain what this means, leading to an original idea (turn 11) that elicits Ms. Schnader's enthusiasm and praise (turns 12 and 14).

The outcome of this interaction, and Dorinda's assessment session overall, was that Ms. Schnader was able to observe Dorinda's ability to self-assess, while also recognizing that Dorinda was not as adept at making her own corrections as Leslie was. Ms. Schnader therefore determined that "revising on her own" and "thinking critically about editing" should be the next step in Dorinda's progression of development as a writer.

Even when teachers do not deliberately make supporting students' evaluation and revision processes an explicit goal of think-aloud writing assessment, concerns about these and other processes, may arise during the session, and teachers may reflect on what they learned about students' evaluation and revision skills during that session. Ms. Denton and Mr. Barquin, colleagues who co-teach 9th grade in a high school that emphasizes writing in its curriculum, found the interactive think-aloud assessment to be a better way of giving students feedback, because their students typically don't revise their work based on teacher comments. Ms. Denton reflected, "I feel like teaching students how to revise is a whole different skill, and I'm not sure if I necessarily know or have figured out the best way to do that." Her colleague Mr. Barquin lamented that students had not really learned how to revise their writing to make substantive changes:

> They need a whole process for that revision. Coming to our office hours, that has to change. They can't just come in, "What do I need to fix?" because that's what they do. "What do I need to fix?" and they just fix it, but they're not internalizing it.

Through their work with interactive think-aloud assessment, these teachers began to see the potential for this approach to support students in developing and internalizing the capacity for evaluating their own writing.

Self-Regulation

Teaching self-regulation is one of the main goals of a popular and extensively studied instructional program for writing known as Self-Regulated Strategy Development, or SRSD (Santangelo, Harris, & Graham, 2007). In this approach, students learn not only writing strategies, which have been shown consistently to produce better-quality writing, but also how to monitor and regulate their use of these strategies. Listening to students think aloud about their writing processes without prompting or questioning them—that is, the noninteractive think-aloud method—can reveal what strategies they use, how well they regulate these strategies, and whether they are able to manage the many aspects of a writing task that compete for their attention in a single moment. When students are writing about a source text, typically a piece of literature in an ELA classroom, these competing demands are even greater. Students have to recall what they have read and scan their memories—or the text, if it is in front of them—for relevant and interesting examples that relate to the claims they are trying to make, so they need to regulate their reading processes as well as their writing process. Mr. Binder experienced this with Tiffany, noting that when she was writing to persuade a friend to read Edwidge Danticat's short story "The Reading Lessons," she "privileged the correctness of the material and the memory of the material" over the "construction and the organization of the writing itself." Mr. Binder expected Tiffany to return to the prompt, but, in Mr. Binder's words, the student "had other priorities." This is an example of how it can be useful to observe how a student approaches a timed task given without prior discussion or warm-up. Doing so can yield insights into the strategies students use to approach the task and how they distribute their effort in completing it. This information can help the teacher prioritize teaching strategies and self-regulation processes that will support students in making more effective use of their time.

Listening to and observing students as they write can reveal strategies and self-regulation skills that may be useful for other students. For example, when Ms. Lindner observed Barbara writing an essay to persuade a friend to read *The Fault in Our Stars*, she noticed that Barbara created a quick checklist of things she wanted to make sure not to forget to do in her essay. This gave Ms. Lindner an idea for a strategy she could teach to the other students in Barbara's class. Less explicit than a checklist, but still useful, are the comments students make to themselves as they write. For example, they may tell themselves not to spend too much time searching for the best word, or make a note to themselves to look up a detail from a book rather than spending time scanning their memories trying to recall the detail. These are comments that can be pooled as a set of tactics for writing and shared with the class.

When teachers use the interactive think-aloud method, they can act immediately on what they learn from observing students' struggles, by interjecting prompts to guide students in pacing themselves and allocating time effectively. Teachers commonly find that time limitations on writing are challenging for students. In timed writing tasks of the sort that students will face on almost any standardized assessment administered at the high school or college level, students need to accomplish as much as possible with their writing in the typically brief allotted time. But even in writing tasks or sessions that are not formally timed, other academic tasks compete for students' (and teachers') time, and students need to learn how to make the most of whatever time they have. Ms. Stanley, who works in an academic magnet high school to which students are admitted through a competitive process, realized during the think-aloud session that one of her students, Laura, tended to fixate on precision in word choice and was slowed down by her iterative revisions of words more than Ms. Stanley thought was helpful. During Laura's composing session, Ms. Stanley was able to guide Laura away from this fixation. For example, when Laura was expressing a need to articulate her interpretation of Eliza in "a more writerly way," Ms. Stanley suggested, "Don't worry about that [saying it in a writerly way]. Can you capture that in your brainstorm so you don't forget that that's where you have to go?" And when Laura paused for 8 seconds and worried aloud that "it could be better," Ms. Stanley suggested, "What if you just left a placeholder for yourself, like, 'put plant metaphor in,' to get yourself unstuck?"

Challenges with self-regulation are not limited to writers who struggle; this is an aspect of writing worth attending to when working with writers at all levels. Time management was a skill that Mr. Tancredi prioritized when planning his think-aloud sessions for the task of writing an essay about "The Rime of the Ancient Mariner." During his session with Alex, a student who aspired to write professionally and had a strong identity as a writer, he noticed that Alex was spending too much time focusing on issues of style and including too much unnecessary detail in his examples. Based on this insight, Mr. Tancredi decided to focus the discussion on time management, which led to the following exchange:

> *Mr. Tancredi:* I want you to start evaluating the kind of evidence that we would use.
> *Alex:* But with me, I like to put a lot of detail into it even if I'm timed. I like putting detail in whatever I'm writing so that the reader can really really grasp what exactly has happened.
> *Mr. Tancredi:* So you have a problem with time management. Do you think your need to put details—
> *Alex:* Is an impulse, yes.
> *Mr. Tancredi:* —affects your time management?
> *Alex:* Yes.

For the remainder of the session, Mr. Tancredi used questions to prompt Alex to evaluate whether certain details were really necessary to the argument he was developing—for example, "Is there a way you can integrate [this information]? Or simplify it so that it doesn't have so many details?" and "How would you be descriptive about that [dying alone]? But try to write it as briefly as possible." In his post-assessment reflection to me, Mr. Tancredi expressed the view that he now had a better understanding of Alex's issues with time management: "He seems to be overthinking questions of style and not concentrating on substance (which would explain questions of time management)."

Language

Language—or what Flower and Hayes (1981) refer to as "translation"—is another aspect of the writing process where strengths can be revealed by listening to students think aloud. Of course, teachers can observe development in students' command of academic written language by noting changes in their use of more sophisticated vocabulary and grammatical structures. But listening to students think aloud can reveal whether and to what extent students deliberate about these choices and, in doing so, reveal a consciousness about language that can be harnessed as a resource for future learning. For example, by listening to Janet think aloud, Ms. Lindner became aware of this student's sensitivity to the political nuances of racially descriptive terms. Janet had chosen to write about Sharon Draper's novel *Romiette and Julio*, an adaptation of the Romeo and Juliet story. During her think-aloud, she verbalized her deliberation about what adjectives to use to describe the African American characters in the book:

> Mexicans and—I don't want to say like, "Blacks" 'cause it will sound racist. But, you know, that's like what I want to write down. I just don't know how to say it in another word. So . . . dark-skinned people, probably? I don't know.

Reflecting on this part of Janet's verbal report, Ms. Lindner pointed out that had she only read the student's essay, which included the phrase "dark-skinned people," she would not have known that the student gave consideration to the political and historical dimensions of her choice of words for describing the story.

Noticing what students are able to do with language is especially important for current or former English learners. Ms. Collazo had one student, Daniel, who was a former English learner and whom she initially characterized as "lacking academic language." However, when listening to him think aloud while composing, she noticed a moment when "he said, 'the old guy' or something like that. He kind of stopped himself and he tried to provide maybe like a more sophisticated way of saying it. And he actually used the word *mature*. And Ms. March learned that one of her English learners' command of language extended beyond sophisticated vocabulary that she suspected was largely the product of the kind of electronic dictionary that many of her students employed to enhance their writing. She was struck by how this student, Simon, reviewed and revised his writing to clarify his thoughts, paying special attention to the use of verb tense to indicate when certain events in *Jane Eyre* happened in relation to one another. Insights such as these can reveal students' awareness of different registers for conveying meaning in academic writing (Schleppegrell, 2004).

When working with ESL teachers on think-aloud writing assessment, I have been struck by how teachers home in on what this assessment method reveals about differences between students' oral and written language. Mr. Clarkson, for example, said that for two of the students he worked with using the think-aloud method, what they verbalized was a higher quality of composition than what they wrote on paper. Ms. March noticed that for two of her students, Fatima and Eva, their spoken grammar was more advanced than their writing grammar, and that for Eva there was also a "richer thought process" and evidence of a greater "awareness of the task" in her verbalized composing process than was represented in the written essay. As Ms. March phrased it, "Speaking is a much more academic language for Eva at the moment than writing." Noting such discrepancies has not been unique to ESL teachers—I observed this with ELA teachers as well—but the implications for instruction are somewhat different. Unlike ELA teachers, ESL teachers are charged with teaching all aspects of academic language, and their students are measured on proficiency in academic language in all four domains (reading, writing, speaking, and listening).

A REFINED UNDERSTANDING OF STUDENTS' CHALLENGES

Insights into students' writing processes obtained through think-aloud writing assessment can help teachers clarify inferences about students' challenges, making them more precise. In Figure 3.1, I present examples of how several of the teachers I worked with refined their understandings of students' challenges and needs. The figure compares inferences they made about students' writing before using think-aloud writing assessment, in the left-hand column, with inferences they made after working with the method, in the right-hand column. The text contained in this figure represents my paraphrase of teachers' comments in interviews and on record-keeping sheets from the assessment sessions.

This figure provides an overview of multiple instances in which the think-aloud assessment allowed teachers to refine or substantially revise their understanding of students' challenges. For example, Mr. Almador was able to get an answer to his questions about Leila as a writer: "What is she thinking?" "Why isn't she able to connect her assertions to her evidence?" and, "Why is it hard for the reader to discern the main point that she is trying to make?" In Chapter 2, I presented excerpts from their think-aloud session in which he used the "reflecting and recalling" teacher move to attempt to steer her verbal interpretations of female characters in *The Great Gatsby* toward a unifying thesis. He learned from these efforts that she had trouble creating a thesis that she was confident was defensible. As she put it, "It could possibly change as I compare [the female characters] but I feel like right now that's what I really have, and I don't know if it works or not." As a result, he inferred that she would need continued support in developing a thesis statement that she was sufficiently confident she could link supporting evidence to, even before working on the links between topic sentences and thesis.

In another assessment session also described in Chapter 2, Ms. Miller gained a more refined understanding of Diana's difficulties with writing supporting paragraphs based on evidence. After reviewing Diana's analytic writing about *The Odyssey* in a previous paper, Ms. Miller had noted that Diana had problems introducing, summarizing, and analyzing evidence. In their think-aloud assessment session, Diana demonstrated that she did not

Figure 3.1. New understandings of students' writing challenges after think-aloud assessment

Student	Pre–Think-Aloud Assessment	Post–Think-Aloud Assessment
Mr. Almador		
Prakash	• I'm just not sure what major point he's trying to make. So, for example, in this particular assignment, it seems like this is his assertion, right? But I'm not sure. Because he doesn't really follow up on it. And even if it is his assertion, I'm not really sure why he's making it. So he never really comes through and supports it fully. So, that's a major problem.	• Needs more help finding evidence to support his points. • Doesn't use text to inspire inferences. • Rewriting prompt helped him understand the task.
Leila	• What is she thinking? • Why isn't she able to connect her assertions to her evidence? • Why is it hard for the reader to discern the main point that she is trying to make?	• Has trouble articulating her thesis. • Not all topic sentences connected to thesis as she planned aloud.
Alynda	• She is not reading on a deeper level. She has some difficulty discussing what is meaningful about a text. • She relies on unsupported opinions about things, and draws conclusions based on those unsupported opinions. • Does she not go beyond surface-level analysis because she is truly satisfied with her conclusions or is she having trouble grappling with the readings, and does this trouble prevent her from deeper analysis?	• Not sure what she wants to say about weather as a symbol; hadn't clearly related F's use of archetypes to thesis. • She did draw an insightful conclusion about tone and mood and connected it to her thesis.

Figure 3.1. New understandings of students' writing challenges after think-aloud assessment (continued)

Student	Pre–Think-Aloud Assessment	Post–Think-Aloud Assessment
Ms. Schnader		
Dorinda	• Does not focus enough on text evidence. • Did she misunderstand the assignment, or does she not understand how to use evidence (because she is often not focused in class)?	• Able to self-assess; struggles with hasty auto-correcting.
Leslie	• Student does not use paragraphs for structure or explain quote source/context. • Was her misunderstanding about the task or a lack of organization?	• Confused about essay structure. • Needed to have explained to her how a critical lens essay is different from an expository essay (the kind she was working on in this assignment).
Ms. Miller		
Carmen	• Summarizes rather than analyzes • Struggles with sentence construction and repeats the same words over and over again (she is a former EL).	• Not having difficulty connecting traits back to thesis. • Struggling with counterclaim.
Darius	• Has trouble picking the right quotes. • Trouble with organization. • Many small errors—missing words, wrong grammatical forms.	• Had trouble with 5 Ws and intro to evidence. • Was able to think aloud and self-assess, walk through the steps of introducing a quote.
Diana	• Struggles with being able to summarize, introduce, and analyze the quote. • Trouble with linking between paragraphs (transitions).	• Struggles with the "I" in the TIEDIED structure. • Has not given much thought to rhetoric (logos/pathos/ethos).

Figure 3.1. New understandings of students' writing challenges after the think-aloud assessment (continued)

Student	Pre–Think-Aloud Assessment	Post–Think-Aloud Assessment
Ms. Miller		
Diana	• Struggles with being able to summarize, introduce, and analyze the quote. • Trouble with linking between paragraphs (transitions).	• Struggles with the "I" in the TIEDIED structure. • Has not given much thought to rhetoric (logos/pathos/ethos).
Mr. Tancredi		
Alex	• Inconsistent grammatical mistakes—wondered if he was not self-monitoring. • Assertions not supported or developed with evidence and analysis.	• Problem with time management; getting lost in the details. • Does not choose evidence well.
Elisa	• Problems with time management: She cannot finish a draft; needs to learn pacing for timed writing. • She uses text as evidence but not effectively, copying whole sections, which takes up time. • Has trouble with transitioning from one idea to the next.	• Implies a thesis rather than stating it directly. • Has good organizational ability—the first part of her essay was well organized. Would be able to fully organize if she used time effectively.

really understand the difference between introducing and analyzing: When Ms. Miller asked for analysis, Diana offered ideas for introducing her quotes. This leads Ms. Miller to realize that Diana has not understood the heuristic that she provided for students to structure their paragraphs: the TIEDIED structure, in which "I" stands for "Introduce Evidence" and the related "5 Ws" formula for introducing: who, what, where, when, why. In the think-aloud session, Ms. Miller successfully prompted Diana to identify what was missing and add it to the paper. The session was helpful not only for Diana, who now had a model for how to successfully introduce evidence in her paper, but also for Ms. Miller, who now understood that this student needed additional support to use the written heuristic tools effectively.

Teachers who pose specific questions about students in preparation for a think-aloud assessment session often come away with answers to these questions. This happened with Mr. Almador and Leila, as described above: He asked, "What does she need to do in order to come away with the main point that she's trying to assert?" and learned that she needs to gain clarity about what she is trying to assert, before she can effectively convey that to the reader. Ms. Schnader achieved a similar understanding after she asked about Leslie, "Was her misunderstanding about the task or a lack of organization?" Ms. Schnader's question had to do with why Leslie wasn't able to effectively select and organize evidence related to her thesis. In the think-aloud session that focused on Leslie's essay about *Othello,* Ms. Schnader learned from witnessing Leslie's uncertainty about integrating quotes that Leslie had been working with another format for the literary analysis essay known as the critical lens. A standard genre on the state high-stakes high school exit exam, the critical lens essay does not require students to use quotes but rather requires them to recall examples from books that they had read prior to the exam and relate them to a short statement. In the think-aloud session, Ms. Schnader had to guide Leslie through planning how she would use quotes, as in the following exchange:

> *Ms. Schnader:* All right, so what's the next step in your paragraph?
> *Leslie:* To add the quote.
> *Ms. Schnader:* Okay.
> *Leslie:* Do I have to say who said it?
> *Ms. Schnader:* What do you think?
> *Leslie:* Yeah?
> *Ms. Schnader:* Okay.
> *Leslie:* And the page?
> *Ms. Schnader:* What do you think? Does the prompt say anything about how to cite it? In the guidelines? I think there's a guideline about it.
> *Leslie:* Yeah, it says use proper citation technique, act, scene, line. Oh, so I have to put the act and the scene . . .
> *Ms. Schnader:* You can see that on the bottom of the page. It says the act and the scene.

Rather than directly instruct Leslie in the characteristics of the quote-based literary analysis essay, she guided Leslie to read the prompt and discern the characteristics for herself. Ms. Schnader prompted her with, "What do you think?" because she suspected that Leslie was a sufficiently experienced writer who, with this kind of prompting, could figure it out herself. Ms. Schnader was correct in this assumption and learned that, in fact, the problem was not lack of organizational ability but lack of practice in incorporating textual evidence into interpretive essays.

LEARNING ABOUT STRENGTHS WITHIN THE WRITING PROCESS

The examples cited above suggest that in addition to clarifying the nature of students' problems with composing, think-aloud assessment can reveal students' strengths. For example, Mr. Almador learned that Alynda was able to construct an insightful interpretation about tone and mood in *Gatsby*. And Ms. Schnader learned that Leslie did have organizational knowledge but just hadn't applied the right kind of knowledge to this particular essay task. Teachers also can learn about how students respond productively to certain kinds of support. For example, Mr. Almador saw that when he asked Prakash to rewrite the prompt, it helped him gain a more accurate understanding of the task. In a similar manner, Ms. Miller saw that when she guided Darius through the use of the 5 Ws heuristic, he indeed was able to write an effective introduction. These are ways in which the interactive version of think-aloud writing assessment can reveal what students can do with support, in effect clarifying the boundaries of their zones of proximal development, in keeping with the Vygotskian foundations of think-aloud writing assessment.

Even when teachers do not intervene in students' writing processes, they can learn much about students' strengths. This is what we discovered when we compared what five teachers learned from using think-aloud assessment with what they learned from their usual text-focused methods of writing assessment. Perhaps the most encouraging discovery was that teachers paid a great deal more attention to what students were doing well and to what they did understand—in other words, to their strengths as writers rather than their challenges. Before using think-aloud assessment, the teachers noticed more than twice as many challenges as strengths, whereas when they used think-aloud assessment they noticed only slightly (14%) more challenges than strengths.

Because think-aloud assessment encourages teachers to recognize and emphasize students' strengths as writers, it can act as an antidote to the deficit models of teaching that historically have obstructed students' academic writing development (Hull & Rose, 1989). The teachers I've worked with gain information that not only can help them enhance their teaching of process—for example, by including more modeling of writing strategies and more practice in self-monitoring and self-regulation—but also can encourage them to view student writers in a more optimistic way. This is one reason I believe that think-aloud assessment works especially well with students who present some sort of puzzle for teachers. For example, if a teacher learns that a student can recall fluently many details from a text while composing but does not think about linking these details to a thesis statement, the teacher can prioritize teaching how to evaluate the relevance of details and link them to the thesis or central claim. This was the case with Maria, a student in Ms. Collazo's class. Ms. Collazo described Maria as "inconsistent" in her writing and either "not familiar" or "not confident" with academic language in the sense that her writing was always very straightforward and lacking in nuance. When she listened to Maria complete the think-aloud task, however, she realized that Maria was able to choose a book quickly and to fluently generate ideas for her essay about the book. Many of these ideas could have been used to support the thesis that Maria had chosen, according to Ms. Collazo, but Maria wasn't able to connect them to the thesis, at least not while she was working independently during her think-aloud session.

Listening to students think aloud also can help teachers assess students' strengths more precisely. For example, when Ms. Collazo initially was describing the student who struggled the most with writing in her class, she made multiple references to his "effort" and his "willingness to struggle." Though admirable qualities in a student, effort and persistence are not skills that are specific to writing, nor are they, arguably, traits that can be taught. When Ms. Collazo listened to Daniel think aloud while composing his essay, she noticed how he directed this effort toward specific requirements of the task. She pointed to his comment that "I want to give the most exciting parts of the film. I want to write about the scenes that were the most exciting or would be of interest," as indicating an awareness of audience and rhetorical situation that she would not have expected from him. Indeed, awareness of audience has been a recurring theme in the strengths that teachers find when they listen to students think aloud without intervening. Mr. Binder noticed one of his students, Greg, pausing frequently during a writing session—a habit he might have considered to be an indication of struggle or dysfluency—but the student's verbalized thoughts revealed that "he took very seriously the idea of wanting to persuade someone to read it [the book he was writing about] without spoiling it or ruining it." And Ms. March, whose students were all English learners, noticed that one of her students, Eva, who was a very recent arrival to the United States and whose writing typically lacked any kind of structure, did demonstrate what Ms. March considered an awareness of audience while thinking aloud. As Ms. March put it, "I could see that she was sort of making considerations about like what she would tell when she was speaking but then what she wrote down she just wrote the summary."

In the interactive version of think-aloud assessment, the presence of a teacher as a listener and partner in the composing process also can provide a context for teachers to assess the student's audience awareness and to provide feedback targeted at addressing students' limitations in audience awareness. Mr. Almador, whose "saying back" strategy I described in Chapter 2, learned from this approach that a common problem for the students he worked with was that they had not managed to translate the thesis that was "in their heads" in a way that was explicit and comprehensible to the reader. At the same time as the think-aloud sessions allowed him to identify this problem, they also allowed him to take steps to address it, by making students aware that they were not sufficiently sensitive to their readers' needs. As he put it, "My asking them questions helped them to remember that just because they know how their point is connected to their thesis, doesn't mean that the reader knows."

USING THINK-ALOUD WRITING ASSESSMENT
TO INFORM INSTRUCTION

For assessment to be truly formative, teachers must use what they learn to inform their teaching. The more specific teachers can be about instructional consequences, the better. Teachers using the think-aloud assessment may use what they learn to prioritize a focus for instruction or, more specifically, to identify an instructional strategy to address this focus (see Beck et al., 2018 for a more detailed discussion). An example of focus-based plans would be "continuing to work on revision" or "teaching about word choices," while a strategy would be to generate contrastive lists of vague/general versus vivid/specific nouns and verbs, and to have students use those when revising. Being able to identify a strategy in addition to a focus leads to more specific support for students. Think-aloud assessment will become increasingly useful to teachers as they develop a repertoire of strategies to address the challenges that they identify through this approach to assessment. Such a repertoire is an important aspect of the pedagogical content knowledge that teachers can develop through formative assessment (see Chapter 6 for a more detailed discussion).

Structure is an aspect of writing that seems easiest for the teachers I have worked with. This may have to do with the prevalence of graphic organizers as tools for writing instruction. For example, Elena suggested that graphic organizers could help two of her students with structuring their writing:

> Maria, I think, definitely benefits from organizing her ideas and using some type of organizer or visual aid before she takes all of that information and puts it into a paragraph.

> Having the visual aid seems to help Daniel as do graphic organizers or charts or being able to just kind of organize the information before he transfers it into a a longer piece of writing.

And Mr. Clarkson considered a design for a graphic organizer that would help one of his students address the problem that her writing was missing evidence to support a controlling idea: "Perhaps the top of the page could be the graphic organizer, and you'd have to fill in each segment [of evidence] and then connect the segments here." Mr. Binder, for his part, had a heuristic that he invoked several times when reflecting on the students whom he had observed thinking aloud while composing: TIPA, IPA, CA, which he defined as follows: "a topic sentence—introduce, produce, and analyze first evidence; introduce, produce second piece of evidence; and conclude like a sort of structure for it—organizational structure within paragraphs."

This tendency of teachers to focus on structural tools when setting instructional priorities aligns with what has been recognized as a broader tendency in the ELA teaching profession to focus on structural aspects of argumentative writing rather than communicative or cognitive aspects (Newell, Bloome, & Hirvela, 2015). I have noticed, however, that teachers who have used the interactive version of think-aloud assessment have come away with instructional ideas that address a wider range of aspects of writing than teachers who have used the noninteractive version of the think-aloud. Perhaps this is because, in the interactive version, the dialogue between teacher and student often takes the process in unexpected but productive and useful directions.

Teachers using the interactive version still thought of instructional priorities that had to do with structure, however. For example, Ms. Schnader considered "outlining and preplanning" and providing examples of "different ways to structure essays" as instructional priorities after she had worked with her students. And Mr. Barquin talked about how he wanted students to do the thinking about structure on their own, before they referred to the outline model that he typically provided. But teachers using the interactive approach also identified areas where students needed more help with the writing process. For example, Ms. Stanley concluded that students would be better off if she built planning time into her timed writing assessments—rather than just assuming that students would plan. And after she saw how her students struggled to accurately interpret the demands of the writing task, Ms. Schnader planned to prioritize teaching how to critically analyze a prompt to determine exactly what the task was asking for. Ms. Schnader also realized that her students were not using the autocorrect feature in Microsoft Word responsibly, but simply were assuming that every change it suggested was necessary and accurate. After concluding her think-aloud assessment sessions, she planned to offer some direct instruction in how to use the software.

Perhaps most importantly for developing students' analytic writing skills, teachers who used interactive think-aloud assessment have had more suggestions for specific strategies related to the complex processes of analysis and revision than teachers who used the noninteractive assessment. For example, Ms. Miller, Ms. Denton, and Mr. Barquin, who taught in a school that strongly emphasized writing across the curriculum and that incorporated explicit teaching of the writing process, reflected on the difficulties students had analyzing quotes in the think-aloud sessions. They thought it would be helpful to have students work with model paragraphs where some of the analysis was missing and they would have to fill it in. Mr. Almador drew similar conclusions about students' challenges with analysis but came up with a different instructional strategy, one more appropriate for his 11th-grade students than for the 9th-graders of Ms. Miller, Ms. Denton, and Mr. Barquin. He reflected that "it was revealing to understand that my students needed more help in determining how they can analyze tone/mood and archetypes, so I would recommend figuring out ways to teach academic vocabulary that would directly improve student understanding of text." Mr. Almador saw that students' insufficient grasp of the meaning of terms for literary elements was hindering their ability to use these elements to construct meaning from the assigned texts.

What teachers learn from a think-aloud assessment session also can help them plan prompts and questions for subsequent interactive sessions. I have seen this happen with the teachers I have worked with: Mr. Tancredi said that in future think-aloud sessions he would work with certain students on time management—because he noticed this was a problem for two of his students—and with another student on comprehension. Mr. Almador thought of a different way to approach the think-aloud assessment sessions after he had worked with one group of students. He said, "I would ask them to look for and select specific quotes and/or passages that they find particularly hard to grasp, and work with them to unpack the text and determine if the text can be used to support a point they have made or if it can inspire the student to go in a new direction." This instructional takeaway was consistent with his focus on deep reading and analysis as a prerequisite for effective analytic writing about literature.

CONCLUSION

Students cannot learn from the practice of formative assessment if teachers do not learn from it, too. This is no less true for think-aloud-based writing assessment than it is for any other kind of formative assessment. As a dialogic approach to writing assessment, the think-aloud method is different from other types of formative writing assessment in that it foregrounds the interactive quality of writing, allowing teachers to discern where students' communicative challenges—and strengths—occur in the process of formulating their thoughts in writing. By attentively listening to students verbalizing their planning and composing, teachers can gain knowledge about students' writing processes that otherwise would remain obscured. This knowledge can help teachers generate more specific ideas for instructional support than they would have using only a text-based form of assessment. Interactive think-aloud assessment offers another level of insight, in that it gives teachers the opportunity to observe how students respond to targeted instructional support.

CHAPTER 4

Aligning Think-Aloud Writing Assessment with Instructional Goals

GOAL-SETTING IS ESSENTIAL IN FORMATIVE ASSESSMENT

As a type of dialogic formative assessment, think-aloud writing assessment is intended to provide teachers with information that they can use for informing instruction—whether immediately, in the form of instructive feedback given in the interactive think-aloud, or following the assessment sessions. In order for teachers to be able to translate information obtained from formative assessments into instructional plans, an assessment needs to be mapped to the particular content and skills taught in the classroom (Cosner, 2011). In assessment terminology, this is an issue known as *validity*—does the assessment measure what it claims to measure? However, the alignment of an assessment with particular content and skills also relates to the conditions necessary for assessment data to yield insights useful for instruction (Heritage, 2010). Having clear goals in mind is also essential for effective feedback, a key element of the interactive think-aloud. Feedback is most effective when it is aligned with learning goals (Hattie & Timperley, 2007).

In discussing effective formative assessment, Wiliam (2010) identifies "clarify, share and understand learning intentions and criteria for success" (p. 32) as a key strategy. Echoing this idea, Maria Ruiz-Primo (2011) notes that, in any kind of assessment conversation, "clear learning goals and clarity about what constitutes evidence of having met these goals are critical in successfully linking instructional and assessment practices" (p. 18). Think-aloud writing assessment is similar to assessment conversations in that both involve dialogues between student and teacher designed to elicit the student's thinking and bring to light understandings and misunderstandings so that the teacher can act on this information. Dialogue that is based on an understanding of goals for learning is what makes think-aloud writing assessment, like assessment conversations, different from other kinds of conversations that occur in classrooms.

The way that Ruiz-Primo (2011) characterizes the role of goals in assessment conversations provides a helpful template for conducting think-aloud writing assessment effectively. She refers to assessment conversations as "informal," but is careful to note that this term should not be taken to mean casual or haphazard: "Informal does *not* imply a focus on the naturally unpredictable events that arise in any classroom, but rather on the small-scale, frequent opportunities teachers have for collecting information about their students' progress towards the learning goals they have in mind" (p. 16, emphasis added). The terms *small-scale* and *frequent* are key here; think-aloud sessions can focus on a discrete component of a writing task rather than on how a student interprets and plans a response to the whole task. And focusing on smaller components makes it possible for teachers to do repeated brief check-ins on a student's progress. For example, a class may have been focusing for several weeks on a particular aspect of writing, such as writing up the analysis of evidence based on notes students have taken on a novel read in class. If the teacher notices that a few students are really struggling with this skill, the teacher may conduct several very brief think-aloud assessments—less than 5 minutes in duration—with those students over the course of a week in order to probe the cause of their difficulty and provide more individualized support.

This kind of contextually relevant and situated (Shepard, 2000) use of the think-aloud assessment allows teachers to make interpretive judgments about a student's performance from the data they collect. It is a socioculturally based approach to assessment, which Pamela Moss (2003) characterizes as "not so much a discrete set of activities, but rather a way of looking at the evidence available from the learning activities" (p. 16). When teachers use the think-aloud approach over the course of the school year, they are able to adjust their questions and prompts, and interpret students' responses to those prompts, based on their developing knowledge of the students. This is a very different practice from using data from high-stakes, standardized tests to classify students into grade-level or other performance bands, where the teacher may not have the contextual information needed to understand why particular problems were challenging for students. Using observations from think-aloud assessment in conjunction with, and in reference to, information from standardized high-stakes assessments can provide additional contextual information for the interpretation of students' thinking and composing processes. And in a reciprocal way, think-aloud session data can help account for students' scores on standardized assessments.

What Goals Look Like

While broad goals for writing are often the most inspiring—such as "students should be able to craft original and insightful thesis statements about works of literature" or "students should be able to write convincing arguments to persuade a reader of the validity of their positions"—goals at any scale can be important and useful in assessment for learning. As Dylan Wiliam (2010) reminds us, goals may be "shallow" as well as "deep." For instance, it may be just as useful for teachers to set a goal of students learning to punctuate correctly—which I would consider a shallower goal—as it is to set a goal of students learning to write original thesis statements that synthesize ideas from multiple texts—a deeper goal—if students' problems with punctuation are truly interfering with effective communication of their meaning.

When teachers apply their long-term, big-picture learning goals to the think-aloud assessment, they need to contextualize their immediate goals in relation to the big-picture goals. An example of how Mr. Almador thought about goals in this way can be found in his work with Leila. One of his big-picture goals was that students be able to articulate "complex and insightful ideas"; when I asked him what his main goal was for working with Leila, he said that he wanted to help her "use quotes to arrive at more insightful conclusions." In this case, Mr. Almador was able to translate his higher-level goal into the more immediate goal of working closely with textual evidence. Immediate goals should always be contextualized in relation to long-term outcomes and considered as "part of a *larger learning trajectory* in the context of unit and yearly goals" (Ruiz-Primo, 2011, p. 16, emphasis in the original). So, to return to the punctuation example: Ms. Miller had broad goals of her students using writing as a tool for self-expression both academically and personally. As a special education–certified co-teacher assigned to work in an inclusion classroom, she thought of goals in a more individualized way, and difficulties with grammar were standing in the way of Carmen, a recently reclassified English learner, meeting this long-term goal. Thus, a shorter-term goal that she set for Carmen was to become more consistent in using correct verb conjugations.

Who Should Set Goals?

When setting goals, it is also important to consider responsibility: Who is tasked with setting the goals, and who is accountable to see that they are reached? Either the student or the teacher may set the learning goals against which teachers evaluate students' work in a think-aloud assessment session, or they may collaborate in developing these goals. Some prompts that a teacher can use to involve students in the goal-setting process at the start of a think-aloud session, or even before it begins, include the following:

- What do you want me to pay attention to in this session?
- What part of this task are you struggling with the most? Why do you think that is?
- What do you most want to work on today?
- For this writing assignment, I've asked the whole class to focus especially on [insert name of goal, such as writing a strong thesis statement]. What does that mean to you?
- What do you most want to improve about your writing? How can we work on that here?
- I've noticed that you seem to struggle with _____ in writing. Do you agree? Why/Why not?

Inviting students to collaborate in think-aloud assessment in this way is consistent with expert advice about a condition for success of formative assessment: the involvement of students as stakeholders and self-assessors (e.g., Andrade, 2010; Heritage, 2010; Shepard, 2000; Stiggins & Chappuis, 2009). In the words of John Hattie and Helen Timperley (2007), "Goals are more effective when students share a commitment to attaining them" (p. 89).

Developing a common language for specifying learning goals and expectations, and a common understanding of what terms mean, is important in all formative assessment practices, and think-aloud assessment is no exception. When students' goals for their own writing are different from their teacher's, or when they have different expectations for what assessment should be about, this can disrupt the translation of assessment to instruction. Consulting students directly can reveal when students' goals for writing and their sense of what they need to work on are different from the teacher's priorities. For example, Ms. March had learned from talking to students in writing conferences that their thoughts about what they needed to work on are "sometimes very different from what I think they need to work on. Especially with the ESL students, there's usually huge focus on spelling and grammar. They're very worried about conventions and I'm focused on organization or coherency or structure or the depth of the writing. Because sometimes they can work on a very surface level." Speaking directly to students is an opportunity for teachers and students to negotiate and clarify their respective goals and expectations, which can help students feel more invested in their own learning.

What should teachers do when what students think they should be working on is not what the teacher thinks they should be working on? Think-aloud assessment can become an opportunity for teachers to align students' goals with theirs. In a situation such as Ms. March's, where a student is most concerned about grammar while the teacher wants to prioritize organization and coherence, the teacher can use the think-aloud assessment to focus on aspects of grammar that support cohesion—for example, consistent use of pronouns, use of transitional linking words (*however, therefore*), and the construction of sentences that make use of the *known–new* formula, a model for constructing a sequence of sentences in a paragraph, in which the first part of the sentence (the known) contains information presented in the preceding sentence(s), while the second part of the sentence presents new information (Holloway, 1981).

When a teacher and students work together to clarify goals and determine where students are in relation to those goals, think-aloud assessment can lead to long-term learning and improvement in students' writing. When students see themselves as having agency in the writing process, they are likely to be more invested in accurately identifying their challenges and in seeking teacher, or peer, support for overcoming those challenges within a think-aloud assessment session. In Chapter 2, I discussed how peers can be involved in think-aloud assessment through collaborative generation of questions and prompts that students can use when listening to one another's think-aloud sessions. This activity can be a productive context for generating and clarifying the meaning of goals for writing. Involving students in think-aloud assessment can help them obtain a better understanding of goals for writing and take ownership of these goals. This ownership, according to Dylan Wiliam (2010), is essential in order for assessment to lead to action, and to meaningful learning, in the classroom. Based on Wiliam's discussion of key strategies for promoting assessment for learning, the framework depicted in Figure 4.1 suggests questions that students, peers, and teachers can ask themselves to prepare for using think-aloud assessment in a way that promotes writing development.

GOAL-ALIGNED TEACHER QUESTIONS AND PROMPTS

In think-aloud writing assessment, goals are most relevant as a reference point for developing a system for recording notes on students' composing processes, and for specifying skills and questions for the interactive version of the assessment, as described in Chapter 2. I always ask teachers who use the interactive version to specify their overarching goals for their writing curriculum as part of their assessment planning. Many of their questions and prompts can be traced to these overarching goals. Mr. Almador is a good example of a teacher

Figure 4.1. Planning framework for think-aloud assessment

	Where to?	Where Now?	How?
Teacher	What are the criteria for success in this task? Do students understand these criteria?	What questions can I ask in the think-aloud assessment to figure out where students are in relation to these criteria?	What questions and prompts will help students achieve these criteria?
Peer	Do I understand the criteria for success in this task? Does my peer understand? How would I explain them to my peer?	What is my peer struggling with?	How can I help my peer?
Learner	What are the criteria for success in this task? How do these relate to my goals for writing?	What do I most want to work on in this task?	What kind of help can my teacher give me? What kind of help can my peer give me?

Adapted from Wiliam's (2010) framework for formative assessment.

who was parsimonious and efficient in his specification of goals and in the way he focused his questions around these goals. He specified two broad goals for his 11th-grade students' writing:

- to articulate complex and insightful ideas in clear and concise prose
- to convince the reader of the validity of their ideas through skillful use of textual evidence

The influence of these overarching goals can be seen in the assignment that Mr. Almador gave his students for an essay on *The Great Gatsby*, as described in Chapter 2. While he had not presented these as formal learning goals to his students, it is easy to see how they could be used in this way. For his think-aloud assessment sessions, Mr. Almador planned 12 questions that he could ask students, although he did not ask every single one for each of the students. Figure 4.2 illustrates how these skills and knowledge align with his overarching goals and the questions that he prepared for the think-aloud assessment sessions.

As you can see in Figure 4.2, all the questions Mr. Almador planned to ask are related to an overarching goal and to at least one of the skills that he had specified as essential to the task. There were two skills not addressed by his questions: "Establish and maintain a formal style, using precise language and sound structure" (9) and "Demonstrate control of the conventions with infrequent errors" (10). In the brief time that he worked with each individual student, he could not possibly cover all skills. Because he was working with the students at the beginning of their writing process, when they were still drafting thesis statements and introductory paragraphs, it made sense for him to defer assessment and support of skills best addressed later in the writing process. Think-aloud assessment is an investment of time, and in order for gains from this investment to be realized, it is important for teachers to focus on the goals that are most appropriate for the particular stage in the writing process and the needs of the students. Specifying skills required to successfully complete a writing task first, before planning questions, will help teachers ask questions that are relevant to their goals, and will make it more likely that even their unplanned questions and prompts are goal-aligned.

Teachers won't always have the same goals for each student, but reflecting and planning, in advance of a think-aloud assessment session, about what to focus on with specific students can help teachers be more prepared to ask helpful questions during the think-aloud, and also can make teachers more attentive to relevant aspects of students' writing processes within those sessions. One of the teachers I've worked with, Ms. Miller, was the integrated co-teaching (ICT) teacher assigned to support students with IEPs in a co-taught, integrated 9th-grade humanities classroom. She worked with two other teachers, Ms. Denton, a social studies teacher, and Mr. Barquin, an English teacher, in a class that combined the state curriculum for world history with the study

Skills and Knowledge	Questions	Related Overarching Goal(s)
1. Interpret the prompt accurately	In your own words, what is the prompt asking you to do?	
2. Write an easily identifiable thesis (argument that addresses a specific idea that the student will analyze and prove in the essay)	Can a reader easily identify and understand what the writer is trying to analyze and prove in this essay?	To articulate complex and insightful ideas in *clear and concise prose*
3. Write clear topic sentences that clearly connect to the thesis	What is your plan for the essay? How did you prove your thesis?	To articulate complex and insightful ideas in *clear and concise prose*
4. Organize paragraphs that convey a coherent argument	How does your topic sentence connect to the main point you are trying to prove and/or analyze?	To articulate complex and insightful ideas in *clear and concise prose*
5. Maintain focus of argument so that the point of each paragraph is always clear	How does your topic sentence connect to the main point you are trying to prove and/or analyze?	To articulate complex and insightful ideas in *clear and concise prose*
6. Identify quotes that relate to your chosen subject (women in the novel or the American dream)	Same as for 8. below	To *convince* the reader of the validity of their ideas through *skillful use of textual evidence*
7. Make insightful inferences about your chosen topic subject (women in the novel or the American dream)	What is Fitzgerald's definition of the American dream?	To articulate *complex and insightful ideas* in clear and concise prose
8. Convincingly support all inferences with text-based evidence on the chosen subject (women in the novel or the American dream)	How does the narrator convey the tone and mood? What is an archetype? What archetype does the main character represent? What quotes support your assertion of which archetype the main character represents? What is symbolism? What ideas do the symbols represent?	To *convince* the reader of the validity of their ideas through *skillful use of textual evidence*
9. Establish and maintain a formal style, using precise language and sound structure		To articulate complex and insightful ideas in *clear and concise prose*
10. Demonstrate control of the conventions with infrequent errors		To articulate complex and insightful ideas in *clear and concise prose*

of relevant literature and the teaching of writing skills related to tasks aligned with the state 9th-grade writing standards. Consistent with her role as an ICT teacher, Ms. Miller described her goals in a more individualized way. Rather than specifying goals for the entire class, she explained:

> I don't have one specific goal for *all* of my students as writers overall. Each one of my students is at a different place and has a different goal to reach. Some of my students have a goal to write a paragraph using two pieces of evidence by the end of the year—and that is where they are right now. Some of my students have goals to be able to identify important evidence to support a claim and write a four-paragraph essay. In general, I would like all of my students to improve upon their reading stamina, use the vocabulary they are learning in their texts in their writing, and work on their organization of their thoughts.

Figure 4.3 shows the alignment of Ms. Miller's questions with the skills that she had specified as necessary for the *Julius Caesar* essay assignment, as well as how these questions and skills relate to the various individual goals. It also illustrates how the questions varied for different students (each question is tagged with the names of the students she asked the question of).

Like Mr. Almador, although Ms. Miller specified control of "conventions" as a necessary skill for this task, she did not plan any questions related to this skill, nor did she spontaneously ask any questions related to grammar or mechanics in her think-aloud assessment sessions. The only question having to do with the linguistic aspect of writing was her question "Did you use effective transitions in your essay to move between paragraphs and from your context into your evidence?" and she asked this question of only one student, Carmen. Notably, Carmen was the only former English learner in the group of students that Ms. Miller worked with, and when interviewed prior to their think-aloud session, Ms. Miller and her colleagues had identified lack of fluency in English as a significant challenge in Carmen's writing. As Mr. Barquin put it, "I notice that her thought process is, I would say, really sound. But I think she does struggle with actually translating the thoughts that she's having in her mind to the page. . . . I think it just takes her maybe a little bit longer than somebody who is or was a native speaker of the language." Carmen was the only student for whom the teachers collectively agreed that focusing on "forms of words" should be a next goal in development, and Ms. Miller's inclusion of the question about effective transitions reflected this focus. On her record-keeping sheet for Carmen, Ms. Miller noted that Carmen still "sometimes struggled with finding the right word."

Their discussion of transitions during the think-aloud session was brief and focused mainly on prompting Carmen to self-assess whether she had used transitions effectively. When I spoke to her after the think-aloud assessment session, Carmen reported that she didn't have trouble with knowing where transitions should go in her essay, but that she "just needed to know the right word to use." Because Ms. Miller and her colleagues were more focused on analysis and organization than on language for the class as a whole, Carmen's more specific linguistic needs did not get the level of attention that she seemed to want and need. However, it is important for content-area teachers who teach current or recently reclassified English learners to know that they can use the think-aloud assessment for micro-assessment of these students' language challenges. For example, teachers can ask not only whether students think they have used transitions effectively, but what words they could use to improve their transitions and make them more accurate, and perhaps can offer words that have been taught recently as a way to assess students' ability to use them accurately. Specifying "using a variety of transition words and grammatical constructions accurately" as a short-term goal for a think-aloud assessment session would align well with Ms. Miller's larger goal for teaching: that writing be, as she put it, "a powerful tool that my students have as a way of self-expression both academically and personally."

Even when I have used think-aloud assessment with ESL support teachers—teachers who co-teach with an English teacher an ELA content class designed for English learners—they tend to prioritize substantive and structural aspects of writing rather than grammar. For example, as I noted earlier in this chapter, while Ms. March's English learner students were quite concerned themselves about spelling and grammar, Ms. March was, in her words, "focused on organization or coherency or is the structure strong . . . or the depth of the writing. Because sometimes they can work on a very surface level." Teachers may feel a tension between having to address discourse-level goals of coherence, organization, and idea development, on the one hand, and sentence-level grammatical issues, on the other. This speaks to a larger tension in the teaching of English language arts between teaching for language use and teaching for meaning, one that, in Mary Schleppegrell's (2007) view, has created an artificial and unhelpful divide. As she has argued, "Close attention to language itself doesn't have to mean a focus on the 'etiquette' of formal correctness, but instead can recognize the meaning-making potential of different language choices that contribute to text organization and interpersonal stance as well as meaning in the sense of 'content'" (p. 123). Adding the interactive component to think-aloud assessment offers a better opportunity to explore students' knowledge of language and ability to use language to express meaning than text-focused assessments permit.

Ms. March did not use the interactive version of think-aloud assessment with her students. But to illustrate how the interactive approach could be useful to teachers like her, I have extracted the skills specified in the record-keeping sheet that she used to assess her students' writing processes in response to an argumentative prompt. I then transposed them to a new template for think-aloud assessment planning in order to show how she could have inserted prompts and questions that would have allowed her to delve deeper into

Figure 4.3. Alignment between skills and knowledge, assessment questions, and overarching goals in Ms. Miller's think-aloud assessment sessions

Skills and Knowledge	Questions	Related Overarching Goal(s)
1. Understand the prompt and understand what the task sheet is asking student to do	In your own words, what is the task sheet asking you to do? (Carmen, Darius)	
2. Use TIEDIED organizer to help write the essay	In what ways did the organizer help you organize your essay? What do you feel like some of the challenges with using it are? (Carmen, Darius)	• Work on the organization of their thoughts
3. Identify character traits relating to the task	What are the two most important leadership traits of your chosen candidate and Julius Caesar and how do they connect to the values of Roman society? (Carmen, Darius, Diana)	
4. Find the quotes that fit those character traits	How do your chosen quotes demonstrate the character traits you identified? (Carmen, Diana)	• Write a paragraph using two pieces of evidence • Be able to identify important evidence to support a claim and write a four-paragraph essay
5. Analyze/Explain how quotes support the central argument (thesis)	How do your quotes explain the central argument (thesis)? (Carmen, Diana)	• Be able to identify important evidence to support a claim and write a four-paragraph essay
6. Explain how character traits and rhetorical techniques support the central argument (thesis)	How do the character traits and rhetorical devices you identified connect to the values of Roman society? (Carmen, Darius)	• Be able to identify important evidence to support a claim and write a four-paragraph essay

Figure 4.3. Alignment between skills and knowledge, assessment questions, and overarching goals in Ms. Miller's think-aloud assessment sessions (continued)

Skills and Knowledge	Questions	Related Overarching Goal(s)
7. Develop a cohesive structure for the essay, using smooth transitions between paragraphs and into textual evidence	Did you use effective transitions in your essay to move between paragraphs and from your context into your evidence? (Carmen)	• Work on the organization of their thoughts • Be able to identify important evidence to support a claim and write a four-paragraph essay
8. Develop a strong counterclaim and refutation paragraph describing why your candidate is still the best choice for the next leader of Rome	Does your counterclaim/refutation support your original argument (thesis)? (Carmen)	• Be able to identify important evidence to support a claim and write a four-paragraph essay
9. Demonstrate control of 9th-grade-level conventions	Do you notice any easy-to-correct convention errors in your essay (capitalization, punctuation, MLA in-text citations, etc.)?	

students' knowledge of language. The original record-keeping sheet appeared in Chapter 1; the modified version is represented in Figure 4.4. I have selected just a few features of the task to illustrate this modification. As mentioned in Chapter 1, the prompt asked students to recommend a book or movie to the reader and provide support for the recommendation.

Sentence frames, suggested in the first row of Figure 4.4 as a way to support students in composing a thesis statement, are considered a best practice for supporting English learners' writing development (Olson et al., 2015). While more typically used for whole-class instruction in modeling possible approaches to a thesis statement or as individual worksheets, they also can provide helpful information in a think-aloud assessment session. When using sentence frames in a think-aloud assessment, the teacher can adjust the amount and type of language specified in the frame to provide more or less support, following the model of dynamic assessment of language learning (Poehner, 2008). The sentence frame also can help the teacher discern whether the student's difficulty has more to do with language or ideas. If, after being given a sentence frame, the student still is not able to complete

Figure 4.4. Modified think-aloud assessment questions designed to assess English learners' challenges with the linguistic aspects of argumentative writing

Skills Required to Complete a Task	Questions and Prompts the Teacher Could Use to Probe Students' Knowledge of Language Related to This Aspect of Writing
The student must come up with a clear thesis statement.	Provide sentence frame, e.g.: • You should read this book because _____. • If you read this book you will feel _____ because _____. • Observe whether the student can complete the frame with a grammatically complete and correct answer.
The student must use transitions between paragraphs effectively to connect ideas.	• Show me where a transition should go in this part of the paper. • What are some words or phrases that you could use for a transition here? • Here are two possibilities for transitions. Tell me which is better: • Another example is when . . . • After the scene at the party, Daisy shows her weakness again . . .
The student must accurately use conventions of written English. And The student must evaluate and revise his or her writing to clarify meaning.	• This sentence does not have a verb. Can you fix that? • The verb and the noun do not agree in this sentence. Can you fix that? • There are three places in this paragraph where you have omitted an article that needs to be there. Can you find and correct them?
The student must identify appropriate words to express his or her meaning. And The student must evaluate and revise his or her writing to clarify meaning.	• Identify a word that did not make sense in the content of a sentence. This sentence did not make sense to me and I think this word is the problem. Can you explain to me what this word means? Can you think of another word that would fit better?

the sentence with an idea that reflects the content of the source text, then the student is likely to need further support in reading comprehension and interpretation to develop ideas about the text, before attempting to compose an essay.

THINK-ALOUD ASSESSMENT AND INSTRUCTIONAL GOALS

There are three prerequisites for formative assessment: (1) an awareness of a standard that is being aimed for, (2) an ability to compare the actual level of performance with that standard, and (3) the ability to take action to move from the actual to the goal (Heritage, 2008). These prerequisites correspond to the three columns in Figure 4.1. Teachers would benefit from keeping these prerequisites in mind as they plan how to use the think-aloud method of writing assessment. Curriculum standards, such as the Common Core or other state standards, or standards established by professional associations such as National Council of Teachers of English/International Reading Association (1996), are a logical point for a teacher to reference when setting goals, if these standards are the framework by which the teacher's students ultimately are going to be measured in external assessments. I would argue, though, that these standards by themselves are not sufficient as a reference point for think-aloud writing assessment, or any kind of dialogic formative assessment, because they can lead to binary assessments of merely whether students have, or have not, met a standard. The problem with using standards alone is that, in the words of Margaret Heritage (2008), these standards "do not provide clear progressions that allow teachers and students to locate where students are on the pathway to desired learning goals" (p. 39). For classroom assessment, teachers need an approach that illuminates why students are not meeting a standard and that fosters growth toward that standard.

The Value of Learning Progressions

Standards specify objectives with the aim of allowing teachers to determine whether students have met those objectives, whereas the aim of learning progressions is to specify the order in which concepts and skills typically are learned to identify the prerequisite skill or knowledge that must be gained in order for students to meet objectives, and to document possible deviations from the typical order (Heritage, 2010). Progressions are important for effective teaching because they present learning "not as a series of discrete events, but rather as a trajectory of development that connects knowledge, concepts and skills within a domain," which allows teachers to "calibrate their teaching to any missing precursor understanding or skills revealed by assessment, and determine what the next steps are to move the student forward from that point" (Heritage, 2008, p. 4). The ability to discern next steps for learning is also an important facet of the knowledge that teachers need to develop in order to be skilled at assessment (Brookhart, 2011).

To show how teachers can translate standards into progressions, I will draw on a couple of examples from the recently launched (2017) Next Generation ELA standards from New York State, a revised version of the Common Core standards implemented in 2011. An important innovation of the Next Generation standards has been to establish what the authors consider to be "lifelong practices of readers and writers," which include habits and skills that are especially well-suited to think-aloud assessment, such as "persever[ing] through challenging writing tasks" and "strengthen[ing] writing by planning, revising, editing, rewriting, or trying a new approach" (New York State Education Department, 2017, p. 7). Managing time, a concern of Mr. Tancredi in particular, is an important component of persevering through challenging writing tasks, and a skill that takes a long time, with repeated practice and feedback, to develop. A teacher could design a progression around this standard by first giving students a time schedule; for example, 10 minutes spent on brainstorming, 10 minutes spent on outlining, and 30 minutes filling in the outline with a draft. Students certainly will vary in their individual preferences for time allocation, and thus the next step in the progression would be to help students define the kind of time management system that works best for them. The third step would be to implement this system with prompting from the teacher or a peer, using some kind of external stimulus like a timer. Finally, students would be able to use the system independently, without prompting from the teacher.

Standards are also genre-specific. For example, in the NextGen literacy standards, students in 9th and 10th grades are expected to "develop claim(s) and counterclaims in a balanced manner, supplying evidence for each while pointing out the strengths and limitations of both, anticipating the audience's knowledge level and concerns" (NYSE, p. 83). This objective could be broken down as follows, in order of progressive difficulty: (1) students must know what counts as a defensible claim and an appropriate counterclaim; (2) students must be able to locate evidence for both claim and counterclaim; and (3) students must be able to present evidence in a way that accounts for readers' background knowledge and assumptions they might make about the evidence. Other aspects of the writing process that would be especially compatible with a goal-based set of progressions include interpretation of a writing prompt; development of a plan for responding to that prompt; and self-evaluation/revision of writing at the levels of mechanics, word, sentence, discourse organization, and fulfillment of task requirements.

Looking at examples of how learning progressions have been used to frame the teaching and assessment of other aspects of literacy can help us consider how teachers may use them to assess writing. There are progressions for spelling (Gillet & Temple, 2000) as well as for speaking skills and listening comprehension (Bailey & Heritage, 2008), the latter of which are divided into three levels—word, sentence, and discourse—allowing teachers to track development separately in these three dimensions of language. Teachers who want to develop a progression for writing may want to consider applying these same dimensions, which would help them target their questions and prompts for think-aloud assessment, and record their observations of students' strengths and challenges, more precisely and systematically.

I find the idea of learning progressions especially compelling when I reflect on Peter Elbow's (1987) claim that "we cannot talk about writing without at least implying a psychological or developmental model" (p. 58); I would add to this claim that we cannot talk about *the teaching of writing* without an underlying developmental model. This assumption underlies research and development on the national formative writing assessment program in New Zealand (New Zealand Council for Educational Research, 2012). This research has found that written feedback aligned with these learning progressions, which include guidance on how to apply the progressions to various genres including description, narration, explanation and persuasion, was correlated with higher student writing achievement as measured by scoring on rubrics that reflected these developmental progressions (Parr & Timperley, 2010). This suggests that formative assessment tools based on a developmental progression for writing can help teachers give feedback that promotes students' writing development.

The New Zealand literacy learning progressions and the language progressions for speaking (Bailey & Heritage, 2008) offer potentially helpful features for teachers wanting to consider a progression model as a foundation for setting goals and interpreting performance in think-aloud writing assessment. Both progressions differentiate among aspects of language: For the speaking progressions, these are word, sentence, and discourse, and for the NZ literacy learning progression, these are the cross-genre categories of ideas, organization, vocabulary, sentence structure, punctuation, and spelling, as well as a purpose-specific category labeled "structure and language." The latter is designed to guide the teacher in assessing purpose-specific characteristics of discourse and language used for each of the five purposes: describing, narrating, recounting, explaining, and arguing. Both of these examples offer helpful reminders of the importance of discerning different facets of students' competence in spoken or written language use. Think-aloud writing assessment goes beyond these assessment frameworks by allowing teachers to assess writing process.

Define Learning Progressions in Locally Relevant Terms

The NZ literacy learning progressions, with their genre-specific designations for developmental process, implicitly acknowledge that the contextual specificity of writing practices requires teachers to negotiate collaboratively their sense of what progress looks like, in order for any progression to be useful for feedback and formative assessment. The variety of ways in which teachers may conceptualize writing development is hinted at by the diversity in how teachers I've worked with have responded to my questions about how they think writing develops. Their answers are wide-ranging and seem in some ways to reflect contextual characteristics of the types of students they teach and the curriculum that their school has developed. Figure 4.5 provides an overview of how teachers I have worked with on the interactive version of think-aloud assessment have described their sense of typical progression for their students.

For some of the teachers, a sense of the order of skills is embedded within this general progression, and for all of them, we can see their sense of what the *sine qua non* of writing is. For Ms. Miller, it is having a strong grasp of content understanding, which is not surprising given that she co-teaches an interdisciplinary humanities class where the study of literary texts runs parallel to the study of the historical contexts for those texts. All the major writing assignments for her class import concepts from this historical context as a requirement for analysis—such as the traits of a good Roman leader or the Greek concept of hubris. The curricular progression Ms. Schnader describes implies a gradual-release (Fisher & Frey, 2003) approach to source-based academic writing in which students are given increasing responsibility for locating and synthesizing relevant texts over the course of the 4 years of high school. Echoing best-practices research on the relationship between classroom discussion and writing proficiency (Juzwik et al., 2013; Nystrand, 1997), she also emphasizes proficiency in participating in complex and nuanced discussions as a prerequisite for effective academic writing.

Ms. Stanley, who currently teaches mostly seniors but has taught all grades at an academic magnet high school, focuses on increasing adeptness with using nuance, ambiguity, and conventionality—meaning such features as archetypes, genres, and tropes in literature—as lenses through which to analyze literature. Perhaps because her students are selected to attend her school through a competitive process and because her student population is mostly at the conclusion of their high school careers, her sights are set on the expectations for college-level literary analysis where familiarity with disciplinary conventions of literature are the primary tools of analysis. Interestingly, Mr. Almador, who teaches juniors in the same school as Ms. Stanley, does not invoke discipline-specific ways of reading but more general analytic practices of students "grappling with difficult text" and general communicative concerns of making their ideas clear to the reader. His clear delineation of steps that students must take to achieve competence emphasizes two aspects of reading proficiency as prerequisite skills: the ability to work through complexity in textual comprehension and to arrive, through that work, at "interesting" insights and interpretations. Once these insights have been achieved students will be prepared to make their ideas understood to a reader. Mr. Tancredi, who teaches in a school for students who have not succeeded in more traditional, standardized programs, is more focused on general writing skills that are not text-dependent. This makes sense given his awareness that many students in his school are more focused on high school completion than on the pursuit of postsecondary studies.

Figure 4.5. Teachers' conceptions of how writing develops across the high school grades

Ms. Miller: I think it starts with understanding what you plan to write about. If you don't understand what you want to write about, you will not be able to write.

Ms. Schnader: At our school, we have a 4-year writing progression: freshman year, students complete an argument paper with selected texts; sophomore year students conduct a self-aware i-Search research paper; junior year students work on Regents exam essays; and senior year students write a formal research paper. Throughout the 4-year process, students work on grammar and paragraphing skills nearly every day. Personally, I think students' written complexity mirrors their complexity of conversation—the better students are at discussion and nuanced thinking, the better their writing becomes.

Ms. Stanley: The freshmen, they come in and they want to just tell you the answer and then move on. A lot of them are not comfortable with ambiguity . . . they can make—you know, they can have a little topic sentence fine, and they can find things in the text fine. A thing that I see is—and even at that level, senior year, they're like, "Oh, here. I found the quote. Here it is. Boom. I dumped it in." But then they just leave it by itself. You know, it's not connected, it's not discussed, it's not, you know, even kind of reckoned with. . . . And then I find what happens, especially with the AP level, junior and senior year, is they start to make the connection. When they actually start recognizing conventionality is huge. So, "Oh, this comedic character is like this one, this one, this one." In literary texts, in archetype and things like that. . . . And so first getting the chops down to really discuss things at length, and then getting the chops down of seeing things in relation to other things. And that's when you can really start saying—being critical yourself. So that takes a little while for them to really see like: What's the ideal reader and where do I fit? Or the ideal critique, and where do I fit in that, and how can I critique that? So that comes later, I think.

Mr. Almador: First [they] need to be active readers that are willing to grapple with difficult texts. This can be done through annotating, free writing, and/or discussion.

Then, they must learn to use the text to arrive at interesting insights and conclusions.

Then, they must organize their thoughts in ways that makes their thinking clear to others.

Mr. Tancredi: You have to be able to narrate, and to describe, and know the difference between the two. . . . If you can't just start getting specific on the most micro level, when you're asked to do it for cause and effect, when you're asked to do it for argumentation, you're not going to be able to do it.

Because Mr. Almador characterized his sense of a progression for academic writing development in a concise and systematic way, it is useful to look more closely at how the different challenges and next steps he identified for three different students relate to this progression. Figure 4.6 displays, for the

Figure 4.6. The challenges and next steps that Mr. Almador identified for three students through think-aloud assessment

Student Name	Initial Challenges Identified (in initial teacher interview)	Pre-Assessment Next Steps Suggested (in initial teacher interview)	Next Steps Suggested Following Think-aloud Writing Assessment
Prakash	• Lacking a clear assertion (thesis): "It may be clear in his head but he has to explain it to the reader."	• Come up with something interesting to say about the text • Convince the reader that that interesting point is valid or convincing	• Focus on one point that he's trying to prove in this assignment • Write down thesis so that he can keep referring back to it
Leila	• Good coherence overall, but at the end of the essay she makes an assertion that she doesn't connect to any quotes from the text	• Use diction, vocabulary, in ways that can help her articulate her point in more nuanced ways	• Responds to her suggestion for a thesis with an alternative possibility, and asks her to consider rival possibilities as she develops her thesis
Alynda	• Not reading on a deeper level • Has some difficulty discussing what is meaningful about a text • Relies on unsupported opinions about things, and draws conclusions based on those unsupported opinions	• Needs to learn specific reading and critical thinking strategies that will help her articulate her ideas more clearly	• Praises her for "insightful" analysis of mood and archetype, and asks her to try to replicate this with the analysis of a symbol, relating it back to her thesis

three students, the challenges he identified in the initial interview; the "next steps" he specified for those students, before conducting a think-aloud assessment with them; and the "next steps" he specified at the conclusion of the think-aloud assessment session. As we can see from column two, the students have different challenges. Prakash has trouble composing clear assertions as thesis statements; it isn't clear to Mr. Almador what point he is trying to argue. Leila has a fairly firm grasp of how to connect thesis statement to evidence, so he is pushing her to attempt more nuanced interpretations of texts and to make use of vocabulary in ways that reflect this nuance. Alynda has trouble supporting the claims she makes and reading for what is "meaningful."

The feedback that Mr. Almador gives each student at the end of each think-aloud assessment session, in which he tells them what to work on next, reflects an awareness of what their challenges were prior to the session and the ways in which he hoped to see them progress as writers. Specifically, for Prakash, asking him to verbalize one point that he was trying to prove, and telling him to write that down, was a way to address the problem that his assertions did not have clarity. By eliciting a clearer thesis statement and assessing its clarity in the moment, Mr. Almador provided feedback that moved Prakash forward along the progression toward making his thinking clear. For Leila, clarity and organization were less problematic, but he wanted to see more nuance, which relates to the "interesting insight" step of his progression. In a notable contrast with his work with Prakash, he is less interested in getting her to commit to a specific thesis than he is in coaching her to make her thesis more complex and nuanced. For this student, it will be more productive, given her current point in development, to consider multiple options and develop the depth of her thinking. Alynda also has trouble with the "interesting insight" step, although in her case the problem is more fundamental: Her ideas typically are not grounded in textual features but rather are "unsupported." He wants to see her learn critical reading and thinking strategies. Toward this end, in the think-aloud assessment session, he supports Alynda's critical close reading of the text by eliciting and then praising the insightful interpretation of mood in *The Great Gatsby*. He then suggests that she try to replicate that insightful reading with analysis of symbol—a reminder to her that she needs to keep her interpretations focused on the text.

What I hope this discussion of Mr. Almador and his students has shown is that learning progressions can provide a framework in which to interpret students' current writing performance, their challenges, and their successes, and to characterize next steps for their learning. Developing learning progressions for writing can help a teacher apply standards—even those that are enacted through standardized tests—in a way that promotes students' writing development. Ideally, teachers would do this in a team, because of the considerable benefits of professional learning from colleagues, but even in the absence of a professional learning community, having a sense of what progress toward a writing standard looks like will help a teacher make effective use of think-aloud assessment.

THINK-ALOUD WRITING ASSESSMENT WITHIN A
COMPREHENSIVE ASSESSMENT SYSTEM

There is no doubt that standardized tests shape teachers' goals for teaching and, at least to some extent, their expectations for students' learning, but think-aloud writing assessment can help teachers work with writing tasks and assessment criteria drawn from standardized tests in ways that defy narrow conceptions of "test prep." The teachers I have worked with on think-aloud assessment repeatedly cite high-stakes high school exit exams such as the Common Core–aligned New York State Regents or the PARCC (Partnership for Assessment of Readiness for College and Careers) as a major influence on their teaching. While not all of the teachers put it as bluntly as Marcella, who said that the class for which she provided ESL support to English learners was "really about prepping the kids for the New York State Regents exam in English," all acknowledge that they import elements from these standardized high-stakes assessments into their teaching, such as the format of writing tasks or the rubrics used to grade student writing on those tasks. Although some claim that state writing assessments constrain instruction and student learning (e.g., Hillocks, 2002; Slomp, 2008), I would argue that preparing students to meet the expectations for the writing tasks on these assessments is not incompatible with broader goals such as, for example, "being able to translate higher-order thinking in speaking to higher-order thinking in writing," (Ms. Schnader), or to "convince the reader of the validity of their ideas" (Mr. Almador), or "to be able to communicate and express themselves" (Mr. Tancredi). Using think-aloud assessment with tasks that are aligned with those of state assessment systems can uncover writing strengths and challenges just as relevant to lifelong writing development, participation in a democratic society, and the cultivation of personal agency, as to the more instrumental goal of success on a measure of writing proficiency. For example, Ms. Schnader noted that the focus of the 11th grade at her school was on Regents preparation, a typical focus for all high schools in the district where she worked, except perhaps those schools that selectively recruited the highest-achieving students.

Although Ms. Schnader taught 10th grade rather than 11th, she considered Regents preparation to be an important part of the purpose of writing instruction in her class. To understand how think-aloud-writing assessment potentially can help teachers support students in preparing for such high-stakes exams, let's explore how this purpose could be aligned with the goals she specified for her students as writers, that is, being "able to translate the higher-order thinking in speaking to higher-order thinking in writing." To understand what constitutes higher-order thinking, Bloom's Revised Taxonomy of Educational Objectives (2001) is a useful reference point. Within the Taxonomy, the objectives, in ascending order of difficulty, are (1) *remember*, (2) *understand*, (3) *apply*, (4) *analyze*, (5) *evaluate*, and (6) *create*. Any type of writing, therefore, can be considered an instantiation of the highest-level goal, create, insofar as the activities of "generating," "planning," and "producing"—the action verbs associated with creating—are taught and assessed as part of writing assignments. As we've seen in earlier chapters, many of the teachers focus on these skills in think-aloud writing assessment. Indeed, the fact that think-aloud-based writing assessment is designed to allow teachers to assess and instruct the writing process makes it a natural fit with a focus on the upper end of the taxonomy. But Ms. Schnader's questions to her students during the interactive think-aloud sessions—like so many of the questions asked by other teachers involved in this work—also alluded implicitly to the objectives of analyzing and evaluating. In Figure 4.7, I list those questions in the left-hand column, and in the right-hand column specify which of the taxonomy's objectives the question aligns best with.

As we can see, most of the objectives that align with Ms. Schnader's questions are from the upper half (objectives 4–6) of Bloom's Taxonomy.

Applying the think-aloud writing assessment method to students' work with tasks extracted from standardized writing exams can help teachers see

Figure 4.7. Ms. Schnader's planned questions for think-aloud writing assessment and their alignment with objectives from Bloom's Taxonomy

Ms. Schnader's Questions	Relevant Objectives from Bloom's Taxonomy
1. In your own words, what is the prompt asking you to do?	(2) Understand
2. What is your plan for the essay?	(6) Create (Planning)
3. What is characterization?	(1) Remember
4. Can you find a quote that shows characterization? What trait does that quote show?	(3) Apply (4) Analyze
5. What is a central idea? What central idea can you draw from *Othello*?	(1)Remember (4) Analyze
6. How does that instance of characterization connect to the central idea?	(4) Analyze
7. Do you use topic sentences? Do you have clear paragraphs separated by topic?	(5) Evaluate
8. How will you explain your reasoning in a way that your audience can follow?	(4) Analyze (6) Create
9. Who is your audience? What tone should you use for this audience?	(4) Analyze
10. Is that a complete sentence? Why/why not?	(5) Evaluate
11. What challenges did you identify after peer editing? How could you fix them?	(5) Evaluate

instruction aligned with these assessments as supporting a general holistic concept of good academic writing. Ms. Schnader's use of the think-aloud assessment is just one example of how a teacher can use this method to address skills and educational objectives that transcend the specific requirements of any single assessment task. Her questions reflect a focus on higher-order thinking that is also present in the *Educators' Guide for the Common Core–aligned Regents Examinations* (NY State Department of Education, 2014), which necessarily framed Ms. Schnader's writing instruction, evident in words such as *complex, intricate,* and *rigorous,* which permeate this document. These are all characteristics that teachers build into their classroom writing assignments— characteristics that the think-aloud assessment, with its focus on process, is especially well-suited to assessing.

CONCLUSION

Developing a clearer sense of the steps students need to take in order to achieve particular writing standards is a way to make writing assessment more dialogic, in that a sense of these steps can help teachers think about student performance as a point on a trajectory of growth, as a moment of *becoming.* As such, it is a marker of both what a student has accomplished and where the student needs to go. Another way in which goal-setting contributes to the dialogic nature of think-aloud assessment is the extent to which teachers and students collaborate on setting goals. Negotiating the meaning of learning goals is a dialogic process between a teacher and his or her students, in the sense that each must speak and listen in order for understanding to be achieved.

CHAPTER 5

How Think-Aloud Writing Assessment Can Benefit Students

PUTTING STUDENTS AT THE CENTER OF FORMATIVE ASSESSMENT

Regardless of the subject area, involving students in the assessment process is one of the most important goals of formative assessment. Early conceptions of formative assessment simply emphasized the link between assessment and instruction: If teachers used information they obtained from assessments, that was formative. However, more recent conceptions of formative assessment view the teacher as only one actor in the assessment–instruction dynamic. Lorrie Shepard (2000) has argued that if schools are to create cultures of learning around assessment—as distinct from cultures of measurement and testing—students need to be invited into the assessment process as participants. In order for learning to occur in the direction that the teacher intends, students must understand the goals that the teacher has set for the class. This is why Susan Brookhart (2011) gave students a more central role as agents in the assessment process when she proposed revised standards for teacher competence in assessment. Among these revised standards is a completely new one: "Teachers should be able to help students use assessment information to make sound educational decisions" (p. 7). In a similar vein, Wiliam (2010) proposed a framework for reconceptualizing formative assessment as a set of key instructional processes, the fifth of which is "activating students as the owners of their own learning" (p. 31). Along the same lines, Margaret Heritage (2008) has argued that formative assessment should involve students as partners in the learning process, which requires that teachers view students as "active consumers" rather than "passive recipients" of the information that the assessment process generates (p. 115).

An important rationale for involving students in the assessment process has to do with self-regulation. Self-regulation is the ability to set and coordinate behavioral cognitive and affective goals, to engage in deliberate processes to meet those goals, and to reflect on one's performance in meeting them. Self-regulation in the writing process is a multifaceted construct that has been characterized as consisting of three types of processes: environmental, behavioral, and personal (Zimmerman & Risemberg, 1997). *Environmental* processes have to do with organizing the task environment, such as location, materials, and resources. Do I have sufficient lighting and a comfortable chair? Do I work better while listening to music, or in a quiet space? Enough sharp pencils, or pens with a comfortable grip? Have I installed Internet-blocking software on my computer? *Behavioral* processes have to do with monitoring one's performance, such as how many words have been written, and whether a particular task, such as revising a thesis statement or locating missing evidence to strengthen an argument, has been addressed. Importantly for think-aloud assessment, behavioral processes also include self-verbalizations as a form of enhancement to the writing process. *Personal* processes include time management, goal-setting, self-evaluating according to personal standards, and use of cognitive strategies. Research has shown that explicitly teaching particular self-regulatory processes of setting goals, using cognitive strategies, setting standards for self-evaluation, and consulting resources such as tutors and books is associated with stronger writing performance (Santangelo, Harris, & Graham, 2016). As the teachers I have worked with have learned, the use of these self-regulatory processes can be both assessed and taught with think-aloud assessment.

One way that feedback in think-aloud assessment can promote self-regulation is by supporting students in the development of particular writing strategies (Heritage, 2008). To the extent that teachers can use this method to make students aware of strategies that were unfamiliar to them previously, or support students in practicing strategies they were familiar with already, think-aloud assessment can support the development of self-regulation.

Another way that think-aloud assessment can support self-regulation is by promoting students' ability to self-assess their own work. Heidi Andrade (2010) has argued for the particular importance of learning to use standards for self-evaluation in the development of writers, proposing that self-regulation should be seen as a key link between assessment and learning. If students can become the primary source of feedback on their own learning, they will learn to monitor and regulate their learning and in doing so will attain greater success in school. Teaching students how to assess their own work is one way of fostering their capacity for self-regulation.

WHAT STUDENTS CAN LEARN FROM
THINK-ALOUD WRITING ASSESSMENT

The Benefits of Thinking Aloud

Think-aloud assessment is not only about teachers' learning from engaging in process-focused dialogue with students, but also about students' learning from verbalizing their thoughts aloud. As I noted in Chapter 1, "reactivity"—the effect of thinking aloud on learners' performance on a task—is a concern of researchers who use thinking aloud to elicit information about cognitive processes. But if this effect is positive, as it often is, it will enable think-aloud assessment to support instruction. Teachers are not concerned with data contamination, and if reactivity has a positive effect on students' performance, so much the better. With these aims in mind, it is useful to revisit this debate.

Research that has addressed the issue of reactivity in the use of think-alouds in writing has noted that the extent to which thinking aloud affects learners' performance on the task varies depending on whether the think-aloud task is metacognitive or non-metacognitive in nature. A metacognitive task requires students to explain and justify the actions taken and choices made during the writing process, while a non-metacognitive task entails simply reporting on their thoughts as they occur (Bowles, 2010). Researchers have found that metacognitive thinking aloud is more likely than non-metacognitive thinking aloud to influence performance (Ericsson & Simon, 1993) on composition tasks (e.g., Bowles, 2008; Sachs & Polio, 2007; Stratman & Hamp-Lyons, 1994) as well as other kinds of tasks (Ericsson & Simon, 1993). Positive types of reactivity include the generation of new content in a revision task (Stratman & Hamp-Lyons, 1994) and the ability to correct errors (Sachs & Polio, 2007). Potentially negative influences include a decrease in meaning changes in sentence-level revisions, the introduction of new word-level errors, and a decreased ability to recognize informational organization errors (Stratman & Hamp-Lyons, 1994), as well as the overall accuracy rate of revisions under think-aloud conditions as compared with non–think-aloud conditions (Sachs & Polio, 2007). Two key implications for teaching are: (1) prompting students to think metacognitively versus non-metacognitively is an important distinction that is likely to have consequences for the effects of thinking aloud on their learning and growth; and (2) because the goal of think-aloud assessment is to produce *better writers* and not just *better writing*, teachers should consider potential negative consequences of thinking aloud against this ultimate goal.

Thinking aloud while performing a task also has motivational and instructional functions. Research in the field of sports psychology has demonstrated that talking while performing challenging tasks can alleviate anxiety and improve performance (Boroujeni & Shahbazi, 2011; Hatzigeorgiadis, Zourbanos, & Mpoumpaki, 2009). While basketball and other competitive sports are different from writing in many ways—sports do not involve cognitive problem solving to the degree that writing does, for example—they both have the potential to induce stress and anxiety in students. That think-aloud assessment may be a way to help students explore the benefits of self-talk for working through difficult writing tasks is one unexpected finding of my work with this method.

A number of the students we have worked with have described this kind of benefit from thinking aloud. Cameron reflected after his assessment session, "I never noticed that when you talk about things out loud, when you think about things out loud it's—it just flows—better." Cameron is referring here not to the interaction with his teacher, but more basically to the process of verbalizing his thoughts. Another student in the same class, Alex, spoke about how the act of speaking aloud sharpened his awareness of the impact of his ideas on possible readers. When I asked him to reflect on what the experience of thinking aloud while writing was like, he said that it allowed him to tap into the strengths of these two modes of communication. "I'm very good at speaking, I'm very good at writing," he said, "but getting used to doing both would be even better." When I pressed him to elaborate, he said that "when it comes to speaking, you can really enunciate, you can really get emotional in front of people and really speak your mind in your actual voice. You can have some emotion to your voice . . . and if you say something a certain way, people are gonna listen." Whereas when he's writing, he said, "You start thinking about yourself." He did not name his teacher as a specific audience in this reflection, even though he had participated in an interactive assessment session; rather, he was describing how the simple act of verbalizing his ideas makes him aware of the possibility of an audience, and how the emotional characteristics of language take on meaning through this awareness. Alex's reflection on the different communicative modes of thinking aloud and writing suggests that the effect of thinking aloud in the presence of an audience can help students inflect their writing with greater communicative intent.

Laura, a high school senior like Alex and Cameron, related that thinking out loud slowed down her writing process and helped her plan: "The thinking out loud part, I guess it allowed me more time like to plan because I usually don't plan as much. I just write and what comes out on the piece of paper is just what's going to be there if it's a timed assignment for school. So, it opened my mind and allowed me to draft more because I usually don't draft a lot. I just write." Laura contrasted this experience with the timed writing tasks that frequently were assigned at her high school. While it would not be realistic for her to fully verbalize her thoughts under timed conditions, self-talk as a strategy can be implemented in subtle ways, through whispering or even silent talk, mouthing speech without vocalizing, as some students naturally do while they read. For some students, verbalizing their composing processes also can have emotional benefits akin to the benefits of self-talk that sports psychology researchers have identified. For example, thinking aloud while composing helped Alynda realize that she had a habit of getting stuck and elaborating excessively on a particular piece of evidence. She reflected:

> I'm aware of that now, and now I'm like thinking out loud, okay, move on to the next point. I think you've done enough here. And it's just like you're talking to yourself and you're reassuring yourself. If you don't say anything, it's just like you have nobody to comfort you in that sense. So you just like, you just get, in a sense, anxious and nervous about it.

Teachers may wonder whether and how English learners can benefit from thinking aloud in English rather than in their first language. The students I have worked with suggest that, yes, they can. Eva, an English learner in Ms. March's class, saw verbalizing her thoughts as a strategy for helping herself to remember her ideas. As she put it, "When you keep something in your mind and just write it down I think it's not good. But when you speak it up like first thing speak and then write, it helps you a lot to get more information or to remember. You have something to remember." She went on to explain that even in her native language, Arabic, she would think aloud while writing. This was a strategy she had learned from her mother: She reported, "My mom teach me that since I was baby. She said that thinking aloud you get more information but like if you do it inside of you, I don't think you get every information you have out." Eva also thought that all new arrivals to an English-speaking country should use thinking aloud as a way to compose, because it would develop their language. As she put it, "I think like most people who just came from their country they should try it because it will help them a lot. Especially English, like we need it a lot because history and math and science we already learn in our country. So it's not hard for us even if it's a different language." Fatima, also an English learner in Ms. March's class, had similar opinions even though, unlike Eva, she had not had any prior experience with the method: "When I spoke and write, it's like, helped me to get more English in my mind. It's like, working my mind. I get like, something inside. It's like, better to talk in English and write." Both students saw thinking aloud as a way to exercise their oral language skills.

Alisha, an English learner in the same school as Fatima and Eva, had a somewhat different view of the advantages of this approach. She saw thinking aloud as a way to generate more ideas than she was able to when she wrote silently, and to make connections among those ideas. As she put it, "I think it's better because when I think out loud, comes in other thoughts, in other things in my mind, and when I speak out loud, they like connect. And when I think in my mind . . . I forgot about all this." Verbalizing her thoughts was a way of summoning stored knowledge and new ideas together in what cognitive psychologists call "working memory" (Pribram, Miller, & Galanter, 1960, p. 65).

It's important to note that not all students reported this benefit from thinking aloud, and that even some of those who saw the positive effects of thinking aloud also admitted that it made them uncomfortable. Simon, for example, said that "speaking's harder than writing" and thought that it would have been easier for him to just write his essay. Jason, despite admitting benefits from thinking aloud, found that it was difficult because, in his words, "as I'm reading and I'm writing, I'm trying to say what I'm about to write or what I'm trying to think of. Like, I kept messing up. I kept trying to choose my words while I'm writing. As I'm trying to choose my words, I'm trying to think and talk. I'm messing up and start, like, writing different and more sloppy." As with all instructional practices, teachers need to bear in mind that not every method works for all students. While I do suggest below some steps that teachers can take to give students the greatest chance of a successful experience with think-aloud assessment, I admit that even with abundant teacher support there may be some who find the activity of speaking while writing to be too frustrating or intimidating to be an effective method of formative assessment.

Self-Assessment

Like another type of formative writing assessment, rubrics, think-aloud writing assessment can support students in developing the ability to assess their own writing. As discussed earlier in this book, one of the core assumptions of think-aloud writing assessment is that the practice of verbalizing one's thoughts in a social context—whether in interaction with the teacher or with the teacher listening and observing—will cultivate the processes of self-regulation and self-reflection. Students who participated in think-aloud assessment sessions reported experiencing a slowing down of their composing processes, which allowed them to engage in the processes of reviewing, evaluating, and revising that Flower and Hayes (1981) deemed central to expert composing.

For some students, as for Jason, thinking aloud even without interaction or prompting from the teacher can spur insights into their own processes and the formation of new understandings. In a reflective interview with me after a think-aloud session with Mr. Binder, Jason noted that verbalizing his thoughts made him more aware of mistakes he was making. As he put it:

> It made me think more when I talk, 'cause I had to think and write at the same time so like, as I'm trying to think and talk, I'm noticing the way I write and how I'm messing up. I kept going back and then I kept changing the words. I kept crossing them out, change it, I read it over and then I'll change it again. So, it helped me notice my own mistakes.

Strikingly, this reflection highlights the potential immediate effect of students' verbalizing their composing process: While it may slow down the process of composing—what Ericsson and Simon (1993) call "latency"—it can help students become more aware of their mistakes and correct them immediately, providing the kind of internal self-feedback that is considered to be an outcome of regular and systematic formative assessment (Heritage, 2010). Another example of an immediate effect of thinking aloud on students' composing processes is revealed in what Janet said following her experience with think-aloud assessment: She felt it helped her generate "more thoughts" than if she had written without speaking, and as she was generating those thoughts, it also allowed her to decide

> what I want to write down and if I want to write it down or if I don't so it's better. I mean, I think that like thinking out loud is kind of helpful because you got your thoughts out and you can decide better which one, what to do or what not to do.

Whereas Jason benefited from thinking aloud in terms of greater capacity for sentence-level editing, for Janet the act of verbalizing her thoughts allowed her to make substantive, discourse-level editorial decisions.

The act of thinking aloud also may produce in students an understanding of their general tendencies as writers. For example, Simone learned that she is "the type of person to think more than I write." This appeared to be an advantage for her, however, because, similar to Janet, the process of generating more ideas than she actually would use led her to question these ideas: "Which one should I write down, how do I put it into words, would it make sense, is my opinion needed in this part of answer? And it's just kind of like a lot of questions are roaming through your mind. Like, is this appropriate for the essay? Like would it answer the general topic of the essay?" Students also may come away with insights into specific strategies that work well for them as writers. Although he worked without any prompting from his teacher, Mr. Binder, Greg learned that writing an outline before drafting a whole essay was a useful strategy for him. As he put it, thinking aloud "actually helped me realize that if I write an outline first it'll help me write better and help separate my ideas more. I feel like I'm being more specific."

The kind of monitoring that students describe as resulting from just thinking aloud, even without teacher interaction, is focused mainly on word- and sentence-level concerns. But interaction with the teacher in think-aloud assessment can make students more aware of macro-level issues in their writing. Laura, for example, emphasized her tendency to lose track of ideas while planning essays and commented that the think-aloud assessment session reinforced her awareness of this tendency. This, for her, was one of the main benefits of think-aloud assessment. As she put it, "I really liked the experience just because of the fact I know what's wrong, like, I know what I'm doing wrong." Asked if this was a new revelation for her, or something she previously had been aware of, she acknowledged, "I kind of already knew [what I was doing wrong], but at the same time it just makes me more aware."

Laura was a senior, but this kind of learning can happen even for younger high school students. For example, Darius, a 9th-grader, learned from his interactions with Ms. Miller that he needed to include more contextual information about evidence in his supporting paragraphs. As he put it, "[I learned] that I need to go into more detail probably since, as you saw, I didn't do the 5 Ws, so I should probably like, make sure I do that more often." While the support that Ms. Miller provided helped him address a problem with contextualizing evidence in the paper he was writing, Darius seems also to have taken away an understanding that this is a habitual shortcoming of his writing, and that he needs to pay more attention to this aspect of his supporting paragraphs in the future. In Ms. Schnader's 10th-grade class, Dorinda learned a new strategy for essay review and revision from her think-aloud assessment experience. When I asked her what her next steps would be in composing the essay that she had worked on in her session with Ms. Schnader, she said that she would read her essay out loud and have someone listen and tell her if it made sense, replicating the technique that Ms. Schnader had employed in the think-aloud assessment. Hannah, also in Ms. Schnader's class, described similar benefits from Ms. Schnader's routine of having students read back to her what they had written in the think-aloud assessment session: "I usually just write without speaking out loud, but since she helped me, I knew exactly what to say, what to write, and how to do it because I wrote my central idea and then when I reread it, it didn't make any sense, so I was able to say it out loud and then write it." This is an example of how think-aloud assessment can have the effect of providing students with not only knowledge about writing or about themselves as writers, but also knowledge of strategies they can use for composing and revising.

It's important to acknowledge that the insights students have expressed based on their experiences with think-aloud assessment were not sponta-neous but elicited in semistructured interviews conducted by me or a re-search assistant following the think-aloud sessions. Thus, it's impossible to know whether students would have experienced such metacognitive insights had we not prompted them. For teachers working alone in their own class-rooms, conducting interviews with students in addition to time-intensive think-aloud assessment sessions is hardly practical. Yet there are ways that teachers can support students' independent reflection following think-aloud assessment: They can require students to reflect in writing following think-aloud assessment sessions, or create prompts for reflection in a Google Doc that students then respond to by speaking into a microphone, using the Google speech-to-text features. This (free!) technology makes the reflection process more accessible to students for whom the act of writing may be slow and laborious.

Developing Awareness of Other Possibilities

As I've mentioned already, think-aloud assessment shares with its conceptual forbearer, dynamic assessment, the quality of being both an assessment and an occasion for teaching. One of the ways, then, that think-aloud writing assess-ment can be helpful is by providing instruction at the same time that teachers ask questions and offer prompts that yield new information about students' capacities and challenges as writers. A recurring theme in students' reflections on how the think-aloud sessions helped them was that in the assessment inter-actions, the teacher helped them become aware of other ideas they could in-corporate, or other ways of interpreting the texts they were analyzing, or other language they could use. For example, Alex, in Mr. Tancredi's class, character-ized Mr. Tancredi's responses as "very helpful because they helped me really think about my responses including things I can add," and noted that some-times the new ideas didn't come directly from the questions that Mr. Tancredi had posed, but rather "opened [my] eyes to other things that [Mr. Tancredi] didn't even ask." In Alex's words, these questions were "kind of a gateway into, like, really looking into the story."

Alex was a senior, but even students at earlier stages in their high school careers were able to learn from the teacher's prompts and questions about new ways of thinking more deeply about the text. Diana commented on Ms. Miller's responsiveness to her statements and how the responses pushed her to elaborate on her original ideas: "After I would say something, she would ask me a question that would make me think deeper into thought about what I just had said. Or like, a question that would make me rethink my answer to add more to it." At one moment in their session, Ms. Miller quizzed Diana about what was supposed to happen in the "discussion" part of the body paragraph structure that she had assigned them:

> *Ms. Miller:* The discussion part is different because in the discussion part, you're doing what?
> *Diana:* I'm like explaining the quote. And I'm explaining the evidence, like discussing it, right?
> *Ms. Miller:* [crosstalk] Okay, you're discussing it, right, and you're connecting it back to what?
> *Diana:* To your thesis.
> *Ms. Miller:* To your thesis, right? You're giving a summary of the quote. You don't want to give a summary in your discussion.

Having demonstrated to Ms. Miller in this question-based exchange that she understood what was supposed to happen in the discussion section, Diana then offered a verbal rehearsal of a discussion of the quote she had chosen:

> *Diana:* Sorry. So I was saying, um, [reading from her text] in this quote, Brutus is showing that he's clever, which also gives him a sense of power.
> *Ms. Miller:* So, you want—good. You're in a good start. But you want to be specific on how he's clever. So like, even if you like go back and you like, reference the quote, like a specific line and you say like it shows he's clever here—
> *Diana:* [crosstalk] Ohh . . . when he says blank, because he's pointing out all of Caesar's flaws . . .
> *Ms. Miller:* Yep.
> *Diana:* —to make people think of him in a different way. And I can say that this gives him a sense of power because he's kind of manipulating the way that the Romans are thinking, and power is a value that the Romans value.
> *Ms. Miller:* Yeah!

Through the questions that both elicit Diana's understanding of what she is supposed to accomplish in the discussion section and remind her of what she is supposed to accomplish, Ms. Miller leads her to elaborate on the evidence she has provided as proof that Brutus is clever.

Teachers can also open up the realm of attention to literary elements for students. As discussed in Chapter 2, teachers can ask questions and offer prompts to focus students on metaphor and imagery in their analysis of text. Almost all of the writing tasks used by the teachers I have worked with were analytic essays about literature, and attending to figurative uses of language in the literary authors' texts was a common goal that teachers had for students. Laura noted that one of the ways in which the think-aloud assessment session helped her was that Ms. Stanley prompted her to make use of the flower motif that she had been working with as she developed her analysis of Eliza's character. At a certain point in composing her analysis she got stuck, reviewed what she had written, and found it lacking:

> *Laura:* I don't like it. . . . I can't get the beginning part, what I want to say.
> *Ms. Stanley:* Well, they meet at Covent Garden.
> *Laura:* Right, okay.
> *Ms. Stanley:* So can you play with that at all, since you're doing this flower thing?

While Ms. Stanley's question did not lead to an immediate breakthrough, a few moments later Laura composed an interpretation that drew a parallel between Covent Garden and the Garden of Eden: "Similar to the Garden of Eden in the Bible, Shaw uses the Covent Garden to give a hint to the audience of what's to come."

Referring afterward to this moment in their assessment session, Laura reflected that "it made me better, because it helps you see what type of metaphors you want to use, what type of language you want to use. You realize that instead of using simple words, you can use more complex words or instead of saying, 'Eliza was in the garden,' you can compare it to something, make allusions." It's important to note how subtle Ms. Stanley's suggestion was. She did not suggest that the student draw the connection between Covent Garden and the Garden of Eden, only that the student "play with" the garden idea, since she had already been working on the flower motif. Subtle suggestions such as these are likely to be more effective in cases where students are fairly experienced with academic writing and the teacher knows the students well enough to gauge whether subtle suggestions will be understood. This was the case with Ms. Stanley's seniors, with whom she had been working for a full year, and some even longer. With less experienced or younger writers, teachers will likely need to be more directive.

Clarifying Thoughts Through Interaction

Students also find that teacher support during the think-aloud assessment sessions helps clarify their thinking and make their ideas accessible to the reader. This effect can occur when teachers play the role of reader and thereby cultivate students' awareness of audience. Although Peter Elbow (1987) is well-known for arguing that audience should be ignored, his stance on audience is actually more nuanced than that. He helpfully distinguished between "*inviting or enabling*" audiences that help us "think of more and better things to say" (p. 51) and *inhibiting* audiences, "awareness [of whom] as we write blocks writing altogether" (p. 51, emphasis in the original). Think-aloud assessment assumes that teachers can serve as inviting audiences for students by supporting and helping to clarify their thinking, eliciting more language and richer ideas from students than they would be able to produce on their own. Even Elbow admits that for inexperienced writers, the practice of disengaging from audience "is a learned cognitive process" (p. 57). To get to this point, he implies, students must first internalize the presence of an enabling reader who will help them generate text when a teacher, or any other conversational partner, cannot be physically present. Think-aloud assessment can serve as the context for such internalization to occur. Recall the graphic I presented in Figure 2.3 as a heuristic for thinking about the functions of think-aloud writing assessment, which depicted the two axes of thinking and communication, on the one hand, and instruction and assessment, on the other. The process of clarifying thinking can be seen as occurring at the midpoint of the axis between thinking and communication: Once the teacher/reader/listener gives feedback that an idea, or the relationship among ideas, is not clear, the student/writer/speaker has to clarify his or her thinking about these ideas, and in so doing deepens his or her understanding of them.

Mr. Almador's tactic of repeating back what students said, and noting inconsistencies or ambiguities, had the effect of helping his students see what was not clear in their thinking. Prakash reported, for example, that his think-aloud session with Mr. Almador helped to

> clarify my thoughts because I would just put an idea and say, oh, this is how I connected. If he was like how does this and that relate, right? So instead of causing confusion when someone reads my paper, that helps me clarify the essay and find the proper evidence to prove that point.

For Prakash, explaining his argument was a matter of finding evidence to support arguments, while Leila found that Mr. Almador's assistance with focusing her interpretation of the prompt was what helped the most. She said that before she spoke with him in the think-aloud session, "my thoughts were kind of like jumbled up and messy, but now I actually feel a lot more confident and I feel like I could focus on the prompt more." As was the case for Leila, helping students clarify their thoughts can have emotional and motivational benefits, insofar as students become more committed to, and confident about, their ideas when they have a better sense of what they want to say.

Students also can clarify their ideas through a process of negotiation, in which teachers give feedback on what they think are the most important ideas in a student's text. As teachers question and respond to a student's ideas, they can reveal a student's confusion or misunderstanding. This happened with

Elisa, in Mr. Tancredi's classroom. She had written the following introductory paragraph to her essay about Coleridge's "The Rime of the Ancient Mariner":

> "An eye for an eye, and the whole world will become blind." This is the most common quote known around the world focusing on the retribution topic. The quote is simply saying that getting revenge on your enemy won't end in a victory for either side. What exactly is retribution? Something given in recompense especially by punishment. Although the quote says that "the world will go blind," in this case an eye for an eye will be a triumph for the supernatural.

In their think-aloud assessment session, Mr. Tancredi asked Elisa to point to the sentence that was her thesis. The following exchange ensued:

Elisa: Um . . . the first quote. I mean the first and second sentence.
Mr. Tancredi: Which one?
Elisa: "An eye for an eye and the whole world will become blind."
Mr. Tancredi: How is that your thesis?
Elisa: Because it was talking about retribution and stuff like that. And I just felt like retribution had to do with, like, getting back at somebody, in a way, and in the story it was talking about the supernatural getting back at him for killing the bird. But, like I was saying in the thesis, it was kind of like the opposite because in this case, the supernatural actually had a victory because they got him to suffer for killing the bird and he learned a lesson. So, it wasn't really the whole world will become blind situation.
Mr. Tancredi: Okay. So, how can we state that in one sentence? So, you have a lot of concepts. We want to be able to point to one sentence as your thesis. Or is it possible?
Elisa: The last sentence?
Mr. Tancredi: I definitely think the last sentence is the closest to it. I want to also let you know that not every single piece of writing will have a clear thesis statement. Sometimes it's implied. And there's nothing wrong with that. But if it's implied, you have to be able to explain it if someone asks you about it. But let's go ahead and highlight or bold the last sentence. So, this is what we're going to work from. Every piece of evidence that you give has to support this concept, that there is some sort of retribution, some sort of payment going on. Correct?

In this interaction, Mr. Tancredi and Elisa accomplish several things. First, Mr. Tancredi assesses Elisa's understanding of where an arguable thesis is located in her first paragraph. Second, Mr. Tancredi takes advantage of this moment to explain that a thesis statement may not be expressed concisely and explicitly in one sentence, and third, the student succeeds at clarifying how her opening statement is related to the larger argument she wants to make. I learned about the third achievement when I spoke with Elisa immediately after this think-aloud session. She described one of the gains of the session, for her, as having an opportunity to make Mr. Tancredi understand her interpretation:

> *Elisa:* I was thinking kinda when I was reading it that it didn't make sense for a second because the way he was asking me questions I thought that he didn't understand.
>
> *Sarah:* Where was it that you think he didn't understand what you were saying?
>
> *Elisa:* When I put "an eye for an eye and the whole world would become blind" because he kept asking me, "How does that relate to the story," so I thought that he felt that it didn't go with the prompt.
>
> *Sarah:* But by the end of the conversation did you feel like he understood?
>
> *Elisa:* Mm-hmm.

Importantly, Elisa's confirmation that Mr. Tancredi understood her intended meaning coincided with her own clarification of her thesis statement. At the beginning of their interaction, she had told him that the first sentence—the original proverb "an eye for an eye makes the whole world blind"—was her thesis. But by the end of the interaction, they had come to an agreement that in fact the thesis was the last sentence, because it made an explicit connection between the proverb and Coleridge's poem.

SUPPORTING STUDENTS' LEARNING THROUGH ASSESSMENT

When teachers use think-aloud assessment, as with any type of formative assessment, they should strive to engage students as learning partners in the assessment process (Heritage, 2008). How can teachers prepare themselves and their students to achieve this important goal? First, they must take steps to help students see them as partners. In my work with teachers and their students, I encountered an example of how a student's desire to appear competent in front of the teacher put some constraints on the think-aloud assessment. After his session, Alex reported to me that his admiration for and desire to impress Mr. Tancredi made it difficult to verbalize his thoughts. In a practice think-aloud session I had done with him, verbalizing his thoughts had come easily and quickly. However, in the actual session, Mr. Tancredi had to prompt him frequently to say what was going through his mind. Reflecting on why he had a hard time verbalizing thoughts as they came to him, he explained to me that "I wanna be the type of student who wants to prove, and being, like, 'I got this.'"

The desire to appear capable and in control can be an impediment to learning in any domain, and is no less so in writing. One way of lessening this pressure is to follow the example of the Reading Apprenticeship Model created by West Ed's Strategic Literacy Initiative (Schoenbach, Greenleaf, Cziko, & Hurwitz, 1999) and make thinking aloud part of students' regular writing instruction practice.

If students see the teacher verbalizing his or her own thoughts, illustrating genuine struggles in composing a piece of writing, and exploring different options for how to work through those struggles, and if the teacher and student work together to establish norms for respectful sharing of writing challenges and collaborative ways of working through possible solutions, this may help diminish anxiety that students might feel about verbalizing their thoughts while composing when a teacher observes and interacts with them.

It's important that this be a routine practice and not a single demonstration. Most of the teachers I have worked with have taken time in class to model their own thinking aloud before engaging in think-aloud assessment with students, and students also had a chance to practice before participating in the assessment. Teachers will have the greatest success with think-aloud assessment if they can establish a routine of regular metacognitive practice in which they model strategies and instructional self-talk, and ask students to practice and model with one another. This kind of regular practice is likely to not only make think-aloud assessment sessions more generative and useful, but also to improve students' writing achievement (Englert, Raphael, Anderson, Anthony, & Stevens, 1991).

Another way that teachers can support students is by providing them with a framework for recording their metacognitive self-reflections. Earlier in this chapter I mentioned the potential of using Google's speech-to-text software to record students' responses to teacher-provided prompts for reflection. What should these prompts look like? In my research with students on think-aloud assessments, I have used semistructured interview protocols to elicit from them their understandings about their writing and about themselves as writers. Based on this work, I've found certain questions to be more effective than others at eliciting students' reflections. Questions I have found to be helpful are depicted in a template for think-aloud assessment planning and reflection in Figure 5.1. Teachers who want to generate their own questions should keep in mind that the most effective questions tend to be those that are simple and open-ended—not yes-or-no questions—beginning with "what" or "how."

The template is divided into two parts: a pre-assessment section and a post-assessment section. It is designed to help students approach the assessment session feeling as if they have a stake in the outcome, and as if they are contributing to the focus of the session by setting their own goals and assessing their own strengths and challenges prior to the session. The teacher can use a student's pre-assessment planning to help form his or her goals for the think-aloud assessment session and also to plan the questions and prompts to use with that student. It is also important for the student, as well as the teacher, to focus on next steps for his or her own writing and for him- or herself as a writer. Sessions should be considered not as isolated activities but as part of a sequence in which what is learned in one session informs the focus of the next. In short, student involvement is essential if the process is to truly fulfill the promise of formative assessment for learning.

Figure 5.1. Student pre-assessment planning and reflection template, for the interactive think-aloud assessment

Pre-Assessment	
What do you think are your strengths as a writer, generally and with this type of writing (i.e., narrative, literary analysis, persuasion)?	
What do you think are your challenges, generally and with this type of writing (i.e., narrative, literary analysis, persuasion)?	
What goals are you working toward now, for improving your writing?	
What goals are you working toward now, for improving yourself as a writer?	
Post-Assessment	
What did you learn about your strengths from this session?	
What did you learn about your challenges from this session?	
How did this session help you progress toward your goals?	
Were there any questions I (the teacher) asked, or things I said, that helped you? If so, what and why?	
What are your next steps . . . . . . with this piece of writing? . . . for you as a writer?	

CONCLUSION

Student involvement is just as essential to a dialogic approach to writing assessment as it is to formative assessment generally. A dialogic approach to writing assessment aligns with conceptions of formative assessment that emphasize student learning as a goal. The aim in both cases is not only for teachers to gain knowledge that can improve their instruction, but for students to deepen their knowledge of content, refine their skills, or gain new insights into their identities as writers. Adding a dialogic element to formative assessment for learning highlights the role that discourse plays in this learning. The examples of student learning from the think-aloud assessment offer glimpses into how students can benefit when teachers make space for students to talk through their ideas and their struggles with composing, and when teachers design process-oriented questions and prompts that elicit this kind of talk. My hope is that these examples will heighten teachers' awareness of how attending to students' verbalized thoughts, and strategically designing interactions with students in the writing process, can help adolescent writers overcome the kinds of challenges that all writers—even experienced and successful ones—have faced at some point in their development.

CHAPTER 6

Think-Aloud Writing Assessment for Teacher Development

In Chapter 3, I described what teachers can learn about their students from using think-aloud assessment, and how this knowledge might inform their instruction. But there is another aspect of teacher knowledge that can be influenced by using think-aloud assessment of writing, and that is knowledge of what is entailed in writing successfully, what makes writing challenging, and what teachers can do to help students overcome these challenges. Taken together, these aspects of knowledge constitute what is known as *pedagogical content knowledge*. According to Lee Shulman (1987), pedagogical content knowledge consists of "the blending of content and pedagogy into an understanding of how particular topics, problems, or issues are organized, represented, and adapted to the diverse interests and abilities of learners, and presented for instruction" (p. 8). While to my knowledge no comprehensive inventory of pedagogical content knowledge for the teaching of writing exists, examples of what would constitute this type of knowledge include: knowing the essential characteristics of a written genre—such as a narrative or analytic essay; understanding which of these features are likely to be more or less challenging for developing writers to master; and knowing how to teach these features in various ways to make their mastery accessible to students with varying backgrounds and levels of experience. Knowledge of how to assess student learning also is considered by many to be an important element of pedagogical content knowledge (Grossman, Schoenfeld, & Lee, 2005; Magnusson et al., 1999). This means that, for example, teachers' pedagogical content knowledge also will develop with respect to their ability to assess whether students have mastered certain genre features in writing, and what kinds of obstacles are standing in the way of this mastery. Using think-aloud writing assessment thus can make important contributions to the development of teachers' pedagogical content knowledge.

Teachers' pedagogical content knowledge about writing instruction merits special attention given findings from national survey research indicating that many teachers consider their teacher preparation programs to have inadequately prepared them for teaching writing (Kiuhara, Graham, & Hawken, 2009). Perhaps this should not come as a surprise, since the teaching of writing typically has taken a backseat to the teaching of reading in English teacher education (Tremmel, 2001).

If teachers at all points on the continuum of experience need support for the development of their knowledge about how to teach writing, intensive experience with formative assessment practices may be a key to providing this support, since research has shown that such experience can lead to meaningful changes in teachers' writing instruction (Berryman & Russell, 2001; Fry & Griffin, 2010). As a type of formative assessment contextualized within instructional practice, the think-aloud method of assessment has much to offer as a form of support for teachers' knowledge development.

THINK-ALOUD WRITING ASSESSMENT IN PRESERVICE TEACHING EXPERIENCES

We know that certain kinds of formative assessment practice—especially those involving feedback to students—are associated with significant gains in writing achievement (Graham, Harris, & Hebert, 2011). Thus, when schools and teacher educators work together to support teachers in developing better formative assessment practices, it will have a positive impact on student learning. My experience working with undergraduate preservice teachers to explore what they learned from using think-aloud writing assessment suggests that teachers who mentor preservice or new teachers can use think-aloud assessment to help these emerging professionals expand their knowledge of writing and of how to teach it. In 2015–2016, I conducted an inquiry with two undergraduate preservice teachers in which I introduced them to the practice of think-aloud writing assessment and supported them in testing this practice in their own student teaching placements. Together, we found (Beck, Cavdar, & Wahrman, 2018) that using interactive think-aloud writing assessment was especially helpful in developing their knowledge of two conceptual tools: (1) their understanding of writing development, and (2) their sense of the relationship between reading and writing.

In the following section, I describe the changes that took place in Diler's and Allie's[1] conceptions of writing development between the beginning of the academic year, prior to working with think-aloud writing assessment, and the end of the year, when they reflected on that experience. I also discuss the significance of these changes in light of what we know about the teaching of writing. I interpret these changes through the lens of the distinction between practical and conceptual tools, as Pam Grossman and her colleagues (2000) did when they studied how knowledge of writing instruction developed in a cohort of new teachers between their student teaching experience and their first 3 years of teaching. Teachers need both types of tools, because while practical tools—that is, specific teaching strategies, resources, and instructional routines—are the everyday problem-solving devices that teachers use to support students' learning, conceptual tools—that is, principles and frameworks having to do with their subject area or with the psychology of learning more broadly—serve as "heuristics . . . to guide instructional decisions" (p. 634). Grossman and colleagues attributed developments in the new teachers' comfort with and sense of competence in teaching writing to their experience with both types of tools in their preservice teacher education program.

Diler, whose student teaching placement was in a 10th-grade class in a high school designed for English learners, and whose students either were preparing to pass or recently had passed the state English proficiency exam, was required to focus on preparing students for another high-stakes proficiency exam, the Regents exam in English language arts. When thinking about what a developmental progression should look like for her advanced-intermediate English learners, at the beginning of her student teaching placement, she considered a firm command of essay structure to be a foundational skill on which all further development would depend. As she put it, "They need to learn to organize their thoughts, to prepare for more advanced writing, and most importantly, because they are ELs, they need to be able to express their thoughts in a coherent manner." After working with think-aloud writing assessment, however, she identified a more fundamental prerequisite. She found that the students she worked with had trouble figuring out what they wanted to say in their essays about *Romeo and Juliet*, and that this confusion was the major stumbling block in their composing process. Reflecting on what she had learned, at the end of her student teaching placement and after she had analyzed the interactive think-aloud protocols that she conducted with three of her students, she wrote:

> I still believe [organization] is important, but not a priority, like the #1 thing to do at least for ELLs, but I think helping them figure out *what* they want to write about, and helping them identify the information they need to write, and helping them develop the confidence in their ideas, are all more important before we reach organization.

She went on to say that she now thought a focus on organization would be appropriate if students were writing something like personal narratives, where they were intimately acquainted with the content of the material—their own lives. But when writing analytically about works of literature—particularly literature as replete with symbols, imagery, complex language, and intricate plots as Shakespeare's plays are—the teacher has to do much more work to help students feel confident in their understanding of these features and how they function in literary works, before she can expect students to write effectively about them. Focusing on structural elements of essays will not address this more fundamental problem. This realization is aligned with findings from research showing that more-expert writers transform knowledge through their writing processes (Bereiter & Scardamalia, 1987) and that writing instruction that supports inquiry processes leads to higher-quality writing (Graham & Perin, 2007).

As a result of working with think-aloud writing assessment, Allie also refined her thinking about the nature of writing development in high school and what should be prioritized instructionally. At the beginning of her student teaching placement, Allie saw the ability to summarize text accurately as a foundation for more advanced academic writing. As she put it, "I think the ability to summarize something that they have read as a means of learning how to write clearly, comes before writing effective analytical and unique essays." After working with think-aloud writing assessment, this belief did not change, but she became more aware of the nature of the challenges that writing unique analytical essays pose for students. She still saw summarizing as an important skill, but she developed a clearer view of what lies on the horizon for high school students preparing for college. She understood that they have to develop a unique perspective on literature, and became more aware that teachers of English at the high school level need to prepare students to develop unique interpretations of texts. As she put it, "Everyone should be expected to write something different once they reach high school." Working with think-aloud writing assessment helped her see this expectation as challenging for her students: "I think students struggle to see or start to grow in seeing a writing task as more individual." Allie's initial belief about the importance of summary writing was well-founded: Multiple research studies have shown that improving summarization skills does in fact lead to better quality writing (Graham & Perin, 2007). However, the change that her beliefs underwent as a consequence of working with think-aloud assessment reflects an understanding of writing as individual expression that is uniquely appropriate for the English/literature classroom (cf. Newell, 1996).

The nature of the task that Allie worked on with students in the think-aloud writing assessment may have had something to do with this realization. The school that she worked in prioritized the discovery of meaning through reading and writing over mastery of form, and her cooperating teacher's writing assignments were designed in a way that reflected this priority. Students had to develop their own prompt for the essays they wrote about David Levithan's novel *Every Day*, the prompt had to be written in the form of a question, and the question had to be a "universal" one, meaning one that could apply to life generally, and not just to the characters in the novel. Among the materials available for the students to work with were drafts of their essential questions, and a set of what were called "inference equations"—heuristics written in the form of [text] + [prior knowledge] = inference—which were supposed to help students generate original interpretations from the text. These requirements, and the struggles that Allie observed her students facing as they verbalized their thought processes while trying to meet these requirements, led her to refine her sense of the trajectory of expected writing development through the high school years, and to see more clearly the roadblocks and obstacles that lay along the way. As she put it, "Developmentally, English can be really difficult for some adolescents because they are uncomfortable with the freedom and the grey areas." In recognizing comfort with ambiguity as a central challenge for adolescents' writing about literature, she came to appreciate how writing in the disciplinary context of English is distinct from other kinds of school writing (cf. Beck & Jeffery, 2009). As she began to define this central challenge, she also became more aware of the instructional need to support students in developing the skills and confidence necessary to navigate through this ambiguity.

Another conceptual tool that Allie and Diler refined through working with think-aloud writing assessment was an understanding of the relationship between reading and writing. At the beginning of her student teaching experience, Allie had stated that she thought good reading would lead automatically to good writing or, as she put it, "the more you read, the better you write." Related to this belief was an assumption that a student who had read and understood a work of literature, and could discuss his or her interpretations with accuracy and fluency, would be able to write an effective essay about literature. After working with think-aloud writing assessment, however, Allie reflected that even when students had completely read a book and could answer literal and inferential comprehension questions about it, they still struggled to express their ideas in writing. She had been struck by the fact that in the think-aloud assessment sessions, both of the students she worked with "expressed quite articulate things, while speaking to me individually, that they could not express in writing on their own." This led her to realize that the relationship between writing and reading was more complex than she originally had thought. No longer did she see analytic reading proficiency as a kind of guarantee of analytic writing proficiency; rather, she saw analytic writing proficiency as a distinct skill that had to be taught and assessed separately from reading. While a student's analytic writing skill could build on knowledge gained from reading—and indeed often could deepen that knowledge, particularly when a teacher provided supportive feedback in a think-aloud assessment session—a student also could demonstrate proficiency in analytic reading and still struggle to write analytic essays.

Diler, too, changed her views on how reading and writing were related. Like Allie, she held a general belief that the more students read, the better they would be able to write. However, after working with think-aloud writing assessment, which revealed to her the great difficulty her students had in identifying literary elements in Shakespeare's play and using those elements to construct an interpretation of the text, she came to see that being prepared to write analytic essays required a *certain kind* of reading as a prerequisite. The writing assignment that Diler used with her students for the think-aloud writing assessment session was typical of assignments given to prepare students for the high-stakes Regents exam. It asked students to identify a literary element and explain how this element worked to convey meaning in the text. This means that, prior to writing, they must have read the text in a way that revealed the functioning of this element. After seeing how the literary element requirement of this task was a special source of challenge for all of her students, Diler refined her view of the kind of reading that was a prerequisite for success on these kinds of tasks:

I think that just reading alone isn't enough. They need to be able to break apart the text, write down a summary or character analysis in their own words, to later on be able to write an essay about it, and [be able] to notice or go back and think about the devices in a book, or think about deeper analysis, especially for students in a developmental stage of writing, such as ELL students or younger students.

The ways in which Allie and Diler refined their understanding of an overall trajectory of writing development and of the relationship between writing and reading made their conceptual toolkit more precise. As I noted above, conceptual tools provide teachers with a way of thinking about how to use practical tools, or specific teaching strategies. Along with the changes they noted in their understandings of writing development and the relationship between writing and reading, Allie and Diler also experienced shifts in their perception of the usefulness of certain practical tools that had been provided to them by their cooperating teachers. For Allie, the change occurred with respect to the inference equation and the requirements for the essential question that students were supposed to use to construct an original, personalized interpretation of *Every Day*. After observing the students she worked with struggle to construct sufficiently universal essential questions, and witnessing their uncertainty over what qualified as "prior knowledge" in the inference equation, she came to the conclusion that "generating one's own prompt was too challenging for this group in many ways. Especially, because not everyone was getting the individualized attention that they needed." She also thought that the assignment "cried out for individual attention because everyone was writing a completely different essay." While she was able to provide this attention for the two students she worked with in the assessment sessions, she was aware that the rest of the class did not have this benefit, and she was concerned about the outcomes for the students who hadn't had the same kind of support. Although in her student teaching placement she did not have the opportunity to make subsequent changes to her teaching to address the challenges she observed, she noted that if she was going to revise the instructional support for this assignment, she would add more prompts to scaffold the analysis.

From working with think-aloud assessment, Allie not only gained ideas about how to improve future instructional support for students, but also learned how to provide in-the-moment support for her students as they composed. One of her students, Beverly, came to the assessment session with a drafted question that did not meet the requirements for a universal or "Level 3" (in the lingo of her cooperating teacher's classroom) question. The question, "How would you handle relationships if you were living an impossible life like A?" was too specific to the novel. Through questioning, Allie discovered that Beverly had misunderstood what constituted a sufficiently original thesis statement and had not been able to use the draft work she had done with the inference equation to develop a sufficiently universal question. Allie addressed this misconception by prompting Beverly to recall the requirements for a Level 3 question, in the following exchange:

Allie: What does our essential question have to be? Remember our Level 3 questions?

Beverly: A question about how your life can connect to the book.

Allie: So what do you think is happening right now with that question? Do you think it is too much in [the novel] *Every Day*, and not enough about our world around us?

Beverly: Yeah.

Allie: Yeah, because we are talking about the characters, right? So how can we rephrase that so we can make it more about our lives so everyone can answer it, even people who weren't lucky enough to read the book?

Beverly: Well, you could say, "How would you handle relationships if you were living an impossible life?"

Allie: Or "How *do* you handle . . . ?" Yeah, that could be a start. Let's write that.

As Allie saw it, saying the question back and prompting Beverly to recall the Level 3 question requirements was also a way for her to compensate interactionally for what she saw as a shortcoming in the inference equation formula that was supposed to help students develop their Level 3 questions. Had Allie not used think-aloud assessment with Beverly, she likely would not have uncovered this misconception, nor would she have realized that with support and clarification, Beverly was capable of composing the kind of universal question that the writing task required.

Similar to what Allie learned from working with think-aloud writing assessment about her cooperating teacher's writing assignments and scaffolding tools, through working with this method Diler also gained a better understanding of an instructional tool that her school used to support students' writing: the M.E.A.L. paragraph, an acronym that stands for **M**ain idea, **E**vidence, **A**nalysis, and **L**ink. Working with think-aloud assessment helped Diler see that this organizing tool was indeed functioning in the way it was supposed to: to help students get started with writing, provided that they felt they had something to write about. But listening to her students verbalize their writing processes also helped her notice something else, that the presence of the M.E.A.L. structure made it clear that deeper problems were holding students back, as discussed above. They were unable to read in the way that it is necessary to read in order to generate sufficient ideas and material to work with in writing. She also saw how one of her students, Cory, was able to use the M.E.A.L. structure as a reference point in working through his analysis of Romeo's character, in this exchange from their think-aloud session:

1. *Diler:* What are you trying to say? Tell me about it.
2. *Cory:* The new situation is affecting Romeo's, it's affecting in the family, in the way that they see him, weak.
3. *Diler:* Oh! How did they see him, you said?
4. *Cory:* Weak.
5. *Diler:* Good.
6. *Cory:* And he's crying, he's hiding, and it's also affecting him because he's hiding and separate from the real world, he's only living in his imaginary world and running away from his problems. Now, how the hell am I going to write that?

At this point, Cory has given a description of Romeo's actions and inner life, without the analysis that the writing task requires. Diler, responding to this as a first step toward a more complex analysis, praises him and employs a "reflecting and recalling" strategy to further extend his thinking over the next couple of turns:

> *Diler:* That's perfect, actually. What you just said to me is, Romeo's new situation is affecting him and his family, because—what did you say? How did you say that they see him?
> *Cory:* Weak.
> *Diler:* And what else?
> *Cory:* Well, that's analysis [referring to the "A" in the M.E.A.L. paragraph structure]. I'm going to write that it's affecting him because—it's affecting his family because they don't know anything about it, they might think it's probably serious, or if he's just childish, which he is, and if they can actually help him, which they can.

Here, Cory refers to the "A" before going further with his characterization. He seems to realize that he needs to do more than just describe events and offers a more causal explanation: "it's affecting him because—it's affecting his family because they don't know anything about it, they might think it's actually serious." Diler then validates these thoughts as sufficient for his paper by suggesting that he write them down.

Hearing Cory think aloud also allowed Diler to see strengths in his writing that she had not recognized previously. Like the experienced teachers I described in Chapter 3, Diler—and Allie, too—learned that think-aloud assessment could uncover hidden resources in student writers. Cory was the third student that Diler worked with, and she was struck by how much more sophisticated and original his ideas were than those of the first two students she worked with, even though her cooperating teacher and Diler herself had seen those students as the more proficient writers. Cory's idea about the effect of Romeo's behavior on his family was a completely original idea; they had not discussed this in class.

Allie, too, discovered hidden capabilities in one of her students, whom she previously had perceived as struggling with both reading and writing. Beverly, whose troubles with the essential question I described above, showed herself to be a thoughtful reader when Allie prompted her to share her thoughts on *Every Day* out loud. As Allie phrased it, "The students expressed quite articulate things, while speaking to me individually, that they could not express in writing on their own. [The think-aloud assessment] emphasized how much both students struggled to express themselves in writing as opposed to speaking." Both Allie and Diler seemed to have learned from their experience one of the essential tenets of formative assessment: that ability is not fixed but malleable and responsive to instructional support (Shepard, 2000). This change in their understanding suggests that think-aloud writing assessment can be one effective way to address what is a common misconception among preservice teachers—that writing is a fixed rather than a malleable skill (Norman & Spencer, 2005). Comprehending the potential of the think-aloud assessment to shape the skills of writers is more important now than ever before as a learning objective for preservice teachers, given that the teaching of "growth mindsets" (Dweck, 2006) is being incorporated into the curricula of more and more schools.

For Allie and Diler, the changes in their conceptual understanding coincided with a more critical appraisal of the practical tools they had been given to use as supports for students' academic writing development. These changes were made possible by exploring the dynamics of students' writing and reading processes. This may help explain why previous research on how best to prepare preservice teachers to be effective teachers of writing (Bass & Chambless, 1994) found that experience with the writing process increased their comfort with and sense of competence in teaching writing.

Deepening knowledge of conceptual and pedagogical tools need not come to a halt after just a few years of teaching. In the next section, I will provide some suggestions for teachers wishing to take a collaborative, inquiry-based approach to using think-aloud assessment to study students' writing processes as a way of furthering their understanding of students' writing development and how to support it. Think-aloud writing assessment is a promising site for teacher-driven professional development because it offers a context for an empirically substantiated criterion for effective professional development: active learning through reflection on work with students. As I discussed in Chapter 5, effective use of think-aloud assessment assumes a high level of student involvement. Investigating how students learn and grow from this method in a particular learning context will provide a rich context for teachers' active learning.

USING THINK-ALOUD WRITING ASSESSMENT FOR COLLECTIVE PROFESSIONAL GROWTH

My suggestions for teachers who want to work together to implement think-aloud assessment are based on the idea of professional learning communities, or PLCs, which are defined by three criteria: (1) that teachers work together *collaboratively*; (2) that their work focuses on *student learning*; and

(3) that they share a commitment to assessing their efforts based on results (Dufour, 2004).

Choose Individual Professional Learning Goals

While working collaboratively is an essential characteristic of PLCs, it is also important for teachers to have individual learning goals related to using the think-aloud assessment. In their review of research on effective professional development programs, Christina Schneider and Bruce Randel (2010) identify individualized learning goals as a key criterion for effectiveness. Examples of individual teacher learning goals include: learning to improve questions and prompts for students, making more space for students to voice challenges and concerns, and improving their knowledge of writing. Or, goals may be more content-focused, such as understanding how best to support students' revision processes or to help students craft more original and generative thesis statements. Teachers should choose a goal that is narrow enough to provide focus and guidance but also broad enough to sustain a long-term inquiry over the course of a school year (see discussion of time frames, below) and to allow for discovery of unanticipated knowledge. Christine Pappas and Eli Tucker-Raymond's (2011) guidance for literacy teacher-researchers on choosing research questions offers a helpful framework for thinking about how to identify goals. Based on this guidance, I recommend that individual learning goals be written as open-ended questions, rather than yes-or-no questions, and that terms and phenomena be concretely defined. For example, rather than ask, "How can I help my students become better at revising?" (too broad) or "Do my students improve more significantly in their ability to revise when I provide a revision checklist and when I implement peer comments?" (too narrow), it is better to ask, "What kinds of support and instructional strategies lead students to become autonomous and effective in their revision processes, that is, able to accurately identify the need for improvement in content and mechanics and make these improvements independently?"

Incorporate Content Knowledge

Using think-aloud assessment is an opportunity to deepen knowledge of content, another characteristic of work that leads to professional learning (Schneider & Randel, 2010). "Content knowledge" related to writing is extensive and genre-specific; to make the work manageable in a fixed amount of time—such as one school year—it's advisable for teachers to narrow their study to a particular genre (e.g., narrative or analytic essay) or aspect of writing process (e.g., revision). Ideally, conversations about how to teach content should take place at two levels: how to provide instructional feedback within the think-aloud assessment sessions, and how to provide follow-up instruction to the whole class or small groups, based on what teachers learn from the think-aloud sessions.

Allow Time to Foster and Observe Growth

Schneider and Randel (2010) note that becoming skilled in formative assessment requires a fair amount of trial and error, in order for teachers to learn how to administer the assessments and how to respond instructionally to what they learn from these assessments. This means that expectations for results from think-aloud writing assessment should not be imposed prematurely, and that patience should be exercised with colleagues who find the practice challenging or frustrating. It also means that time is better spent in smaller increments spread out over a long period of time than in just a few day-long workshops scheduled in close proximity. It is advisable to frontload a longer amount of time at the beginning of the period allotted for professional development because it will take some time for teachers to familiarize themselves with the methods of think-aloud writing assessment.

Create Structures for Collaboration

Collaboration is especially important for developing ease and skill in using think-aloud writing assessment, for several reasons. First, in most schools a team of ELA teachers typically includes members with varying degrees and kinds of teaching experience and content-specific training. For example, some teachers may be skilled and even published writers, while other teachers may feel less comfortable with the regular practice of writing. Collaboration is an opportunity for the less experienced to learn from the more experienced, as is typical in a community-of-practice model of learning (Wenger, 1998). Second, working with teachers across grade levels is essential for constructing and refining a local, contextualized learning progression—a map of students' writing development. Teachers of upper grades will have a better sense of what students need to be able to accomplish with writing by the time they graduate from high school or middle school, while teachers of lower grades have a better sense of the full range of skills with which students enter the school. Familiarity with the profiles of learners at both ends of the developmental continuum in a particular context is essential for mapping a progression that can be used to design tasks, including interactive prompts and questions, for think-aloud writing assessment, and for using the findings from assessments to plan subsequent instructional actions. Third, because think-aloud writing assessment lends itself to individualization, typically unfolding in a spontaneous and "interactionist" manner, it is likely to yield a wide variety of information about student writers, resulting in a multitude of profiles. Any teacher who uses think-aloud writing assessment will likely benefit from the practice of comparing and contrasting findings with other teachers who may have similar students in their classrooms. In this respect, collaborative teacher inquiry based on analysis of think-aloud writing assessment data and practices would benefit from following best practices in qualitative teacher research, where teacher-researchers use professional peers as a resource to deepen their learning and to become "better" as teachers (Lytle, 2008).

Create Coherence with Existing Initiatives and Priorities

Developing a practice with think-aloud writing assessment should build on what teachers already know and can do, on knowledge they already have, and/or on resources they have already developed. The flexible and open-ended nature of think-aloud assessment, as a method, means that it can be integrated with a range of instructional programs. For example, if a school or district has already invested in professional development related to the teaching of writing strategies (Santangelo et al., 2007), or the more grammatically focused Writing Revolution method (Hochman & Wexler, 2017), think-aloud assessment tasks, questions, and prompts can be designed to elicit information about how well students have internalized the skills and knowledge taught by these programs. If a school has made preparation for standardized high-stakes exams a priority, think-aloud assessment can be carried out in a way that supports this goal in a way that is not reductive, boilerplate "test-prep," as I showed in Chapter 4 with the example of Ms. Schnader.

Of course, administrative support is necessary for most of the above characteristics to be realized. Teachers seeking support for this work from their administration may want to point out that these prerequisites for collaborative work with the think-aloud assessment are supported by a synthesis of research across various types of schools and content areas. To aid teacher teams in planning, I offer a template (Figure 6.1) that includes space for mapping alignment with existing school priorities, individual teacher goals, and interim assessments to monitor the progress of students' writing as a result of working with think-aloud assessment.

As I've emphasized throughout this book, the great value of think-aloud writing assessment is that it focuses on writing *process* as well as product; teachers gain insight into aspects of students' writing that would not be visible from reading the papers alone. However, what matters to students, their families, and other stakeholders is whether students become the kinds of writers who produce better writing. Even though teachers are uniquely positioned to have insight into their students' unique processes, strengths, and challenges as writers, they need to be able to relate those insights to the writing that students produce. It is important for teachers to plan some way of tracking improvements in writing parallel to their efforts to improve their teaching through think-aloud writing assessment. The far-right column of the template in Figure 6.1 provides space for teachers to specify the criteria they will use to evaluate students' writing and, if it's relevant to the teachers' learning goals, their writing processes. The criteria should be the same for each interim assessment writing task, although the criteria could be different for different teachers, if the school context allowed for such customized assessment.

If think-aloud writing assessment is to reach its full potential as a method of assessment for learning, the following requirements, which Rick Stiggins (2010) specifies as conditions for assessment for learning, must be met:

1. Assessment processes and results serve clear and appropriate purposes.
2. Assessments reflect clear and valued learning targets.
3. Learning targets are translated into assessments that yield accurate results.
4. Assessment results are managed well and communicated effectively.
5. Students are involved in their own assessment. (p. 244)

These requirements establish a clear and full agenda for any professional learning community that aims to use think-aloud writing assessment. Defining the purposes for think-aloud writing assessment, clarifying the learning targets, adapting the assessment questions and record-keeping methods to align with those targets, and developing routines for involving students and protocols for communicating teachers' insights are all practices that can help teachers expand their knowledge of writing and writers while using think-aloud writing assessment.

CONCLUSION: THE DIALOGIC EVOLUTION OF TEACHER KNOWLEDGE

In a 1921 interview with Latrobe Carroll in the magazine *The Bookman,* Willa Cather stated that "it takes a great deal of experience to become natural" as a writer (Bohlke, 1986, p. 21). Thankfully, the belief that a student's achievement in writing is due to natural talent or innate ability has now been recognized as detrimental to students' learning and indeed to the entire endeavor of teaching, no less so in writing than in other domains of knowledge and skill. Cather's reflection on becoming a natural writer reminds us of a special challenge for the teacher of writing, as compared with the teacher of, say, mathematics or science: The practice of writing does not have discrete components of knowledge that can be identified for teaching and mastery, and in most cases a teacher has an opportunity to know students as writers only during a short period in the development of their practice, one episode in a long narrative. As students progress through their schooling, and beyond schooling into the workplace, the writing tasks they will have to complete become more complex and more differentiated, with requirements that are increasingly specialized and unique to particular contexts. One is never done becoming a writer.

Typical approaches to classroom writing assessment are not designed to acknowledge this reality, nor are they capable of doing so. Not even the most multifaceted of multi-trait analytic rubrics is up to this task. The dialogic perspective inherent in think-aloud writing assessment, however, assumes that assessment is part of an ongoing process of development. It is incumbent on teachers to provide students with the kinds of writing experiences most

Figure 6.1. Template for planning teachers' work with think-aloud assessment

	School-Level Priorities:		
1.			
2.			
3.			

		INTERIM ASSESSMENTS OF STUDENT WRITING DEVELOPMENT	
Individual Teacher Learning Goals	**Relevant Content Knowledge**	**Assessment Dates**	**Assessment Criteria** (same for each date; potentially different for each teacher, depending on teacher learning goals)
Teacher A:	Teacher A:	Interim Assessment #1:	Process:
		Interim Assessment #2:	Product:
		Interim Assessment #3:	
Teacher B:	Teacher B:	Interim Assessment #1:	Process:
		Interim Assessment #2:	Product:
		Interim Assessment #3:	
Teacher C:	Teacher C:	Interim Assessment #1:	Process:
		Interim Assessment #2:	Product:
		Interim Assessment #3:	
Teacher D:	Teacher D:	Interim Assessment #1:	Process:
		Interim Assessment #2:	Product:
		Interim Assessment #3:	

Figure 6.1. Template for planning teachers' work with think-aloud writing assessment (continued)

		INTERIM ASSESSMENTS OF STUDENT WRITING DEVELOPMENT	
Individual Teacher Learning Goals	**Relevant Content Knowledge**	**Assessment Dates**	**Assessment Criteria** (same for each date; potentially different for each teacher, depending on teacher learning goals)
Teacher E:	Teacher E:	Interim Assessment #1: Interim Assessment #2: Interim Assessment #3:	Process: Product:

conducive to development. Teachers can use the think-aloud sessions to observe what students are capable of doing with support, and what they therefore may soon be able to do independently (Vygotsky, 1978). In doing so they may find that their own practice of teaching writing will evolve. As a teacher realizes that a student's "finished" written work may obscure understanding or knowledge that is not yet ready to be committed to print, the teacher will be challenged to develop ways of helping the student elicit that knowledge with the tools of written language. In this way, the challenges and achievements that students present in their writing development push teachers to grow in their teaching. The development of the student writer and the development of the teacher are inherently intertwined.

The idea of an interactional approach to writing assessment may strike some readers as incompatible with the notion of individual authorship and the commitment to cultivating students' unique voices. But in fact, the assumption that writers learn from other writers as well as from hearing the feedback of readers underlies many practices that are now taken for granted as effective and exemplary ways of teaching writing and reading, such as the use of peer workshops and peer editing, the analysis and emulation of mentor texts, and apprenticeship models of teaching. If writing is indeed a social practice, then teachers should have the opportunity to assess writing through interactions that make this social practice visible. One of the most obvious ways they can do this is by modeling possible reader responses in the think-aloud assessment. The problem of the teacher-as-sole-reader of students' classroom writing has been lamented by some experts in writing development, such as James Britton (Britton, Burgess, Martin, McLeod, & Rosen, 1975) and more recent proponents of authentic assessment of writing (Sisserson, Manning, Knepler, & Joliffe, 2002). However, teachers are also capable of being flexible in their responses to student writing and assuming different reader identities—for example, pretending to be a reader who does not know everything the student knows about a source text. In doing so, through this type of dialogic assessment a teacher can be liberated from the identity of grader who audits students' compliance with the requirements of an assignment.

Just as becoming a writer involves learning from other writers, becoming a teacher of writing involves learning from students, as well as from other teachers of writing. A dialogic approach to assessment views assessment as inseparable from an ongoing process of learning, not only for the students but also for the teachers. This conception of the link between assessment and teacher development is a radical departure from the accountability model so prevalent now, in the early 21st century, which views evidence of student achievement in literacy as a variable dependent on, and an empirical indicator of, teacher skill. A dialogic view of writing assessment, in contrast, sees evidence obtained through assessment as an opportunity for teacher learning as well as student learning. By accessing students' writing processes through the think-aloud method of writing assessment, teachers obtain evidence of student difficulties and student resources that they would not be able to gather in other ways and that can serve as a rationale for changing their instructional routines. In situations where teachers are called upon to implement standardized writing curricula, for example, they will be better able to discern whether, and in what ways, these curricula are working to foster students' writing development, and if they are not working, teachers will have a warrant for modifying or even resisting these curricula. In this way, the method can empower teachers as decisionmakers in their classrooms because it will allow them to understand students better and fine-tune their assignments and their instruction to more closely align with their students' strengths, challenges, and learning goals.

NOTE

1. Note that for Allie and Diler I use their real names, rather than pseudonyms as for all other teachers and students mentioned in this book.

Research Methodology

The examples, claims, and suggestions made in this book derive from two related research studies designed to explore the potential for listening to students think aloud about their composing processes as a method of formative assessment. Specifically, the studies investigated the following: whether and to what extent teachers gain new information about students' strengths and challenges as writers, as compared with the typical text-focused types of writing assessment; whether and to what extent this information helped them set meaningful instructional priorities; and what students took away from this method.

DESIGN OF THE RESEARCH

Phase 1: The first study involved teachers using a noninteractive think-aloud method in which they listened to students think aloud while composing a prompt that my colleagues and I provided. The purpose of this study was to explore what teachers learned from listening to students think aloud while composing that was different from what they learned from only looking at students' writing.

The specific research questions that we addressed in this phase were:

- What do teachers learn from the think-aloud protocol (TAP) assessment that they do not learn from the students' writing alone?
- To what extent and in what ways does the TAP assessment encourage a greater focus on students' strengths as writers?
- To what extent do ESL and ELA teachers differ in their use of the TAP assessment?
- What ideas for instruction do teachers get from using the TAP assessment?
- To what extent were the instructional priorities the teachers set responsive to the student challenges they identified?
- To what extent was the responsiveness of teachers' instructional priorities different before and after using the TAP assessment?

Phase 2: The second study was based on one of the findings from the first, that teachers wanted more opportunity to interact with the students during the think-aloud process, and from literature on the think-aloud method that suggests that teacher prompting for explanation can yield important information that only asking students to verbally report their thoughts cannot. The second study also was influenced by research literature on the method of dynamic assessment in language learning (Poehner, 2008) and in writing (Shrestha & Coffin, 2012). I designed the interactive think-aloud assessment according to the central principle of dynamic assessment: that assessment and instruction should be intertwined (Lantolf, 2009).

Questions addressed in this phase include:

- What do preservice teachers learn about student writing and students' writing processes from using a dialogic, interactive think-aloud writing assessment?
- How do ELA teachers use the interactive think-aloud assessment to mediate students' performance as writers?
- What are the consequences of teachers' mediational moves in the interactive think-aloud assessment for students' composing processes?
- What do students learn about writing and about themselves as writers from teachers' mediation in the interactive think-aloud assessment?
- To what extent and in what ways do teacher mediational moves engage students as partners in constructing and solving problems during the composing process?
- What do teachers learn about students' writing and about students as writers from using the interactive think-aloud assessment?

Context and Participants

Phase 1 was conducted in three schools in the same large metropolitan school district. The percentage of students eligible for free/reduced-price lunch in these schools ranged from 59% to 86%, and the percentage of ELs from 6% to 17%. From two of these schools, we had two teachers participating, and from one of the schools we had one teacher participating, for a total of five teachers. Three of the teachers were ELA teachers, and two of the teachers—both of whom taught in the school with the highest percentage (17%) of ELs—were ESL teachers. Three students from each teacher's class participated, for a total of 5 teachers and 15 students.

Phase 2 was conducted in four schools in two different school districts, one the same large metropolitan district that was the context for the research in Phase 1, and one smaller urban district. All of the five teachers in Phase 2 were ELA teachers; one taught in a 9th-grade classroom, one taught in a 10th-grade classroom, one taught 11th grade, and two taught seniors. Two teachers, the 11th-grade teacher and one of the 12th-grade teachers, worked in the same school. Each teacher worked with three students in a think-aloud assessment session.

Data Collection

Data collection methods were similar for Phase 1 and Phase 2 and consisted of these three steps:

Step 1 was a pre-assessment interview with both teachers and students. These interviews were conducted separately by either me or a graduate research assistant, and made use of a semistructured protocol to elicit background information as follows: (a) students were asked about their experience with writing instruction, their sense of their own challenges with writing, and the kinds of instructional support they found most helpful—and in this interview we also trained the students in the practice of thinking aloud while composing; (b) teachers were asked about their instructional priorities for teaching writing at their particular grade level, their professional training in the teaching of writing, their understanding of how writing develops, and their sense of the particular strengths and challenges of each student whom they had selected to work with. In the Phase 2 teacher interviews, we also advised the teachers on how to design the record-keeping sheets for the interactive think-aloud assessment. Several doctoral students assisted me with data collection. These interviews were audio recorded and transcribed.

Step 2 consisted of the actual think-aloud assessment sessions. In Phase 1, these sessions were not interactive: Teachers listened to students thinking aloud while composing and took notes on a record-keeping sheet that we provided (depicted in Chapter 1). The writing task that students used for the assessment also was standardized and provided by the researchers, because we were focused on a specific type of writing—analytic writing about literature. All sessions lasted roughly 30 minutes. In Phase 2, the think-aloud assessments were interactive, and teachers prepared, in advance, a set of questions and prompts designed to determine whether students were having trouble with the skills and knowledge required for this assignment. Another difference between Phase 1 and Phase 2 was that the tasks came from the teachers' planned writing curriculum; we did not introduce a separate assignment for the assessment. A final difference was that, in keeping with the less standardized nature of the think-aloud assessment task, the duration of the assessment session varied across the teachers, ranging from 15 minutes to as long as 45 minutes. Like the interviews from Step 1, these think-aloud assessment sessions were audio recorded and transcribed.

Step 3 was concerned with collection of post-assessment reflections, to investigate what students and teachers had learned from these sessions about the students' writing and about the students as writers. In both phases, we interviewed the students immediately after the assessment sessions, again using a semistructured interview protocol. To capture the teachers' reflections, in

Phase 1 we interviewed them immediately after the assessment sessions; in Phase 2, because of time constraints, we asked them to complete an open-ended written survey. The survey asked them to reflect on what they had learned about the students as writers from working with the think-aloud assessment and how this would inform their instruction. We supplemented these written questionnaires with follow-up questions as needed. These interviews also were audio recorded and transcribed.

Data Analysis

Data analysis for these two phases was iterative and interdependent. Phase 1 analysis involved coding the transcripts using a scheme for categorizing students' challenges with academic writing that had been developed in a previous study (Beck, Llosa, & Fredrick, 2013), along with codes that were inductively generated to characterize aspects of writing not measured in the prior research. An additional code label of "strength" or "challenge" was added to indicate whether students had strengths or challenges in relation to this aspect of writing. To address the question about teacher instructional priorities that ensued from the assessment sessions, we also coded the teacher interviews for the categories of "instructional focus" and "instructional strategy." The codebook for this phase of data analysis is presented below. Coding for this session was done by hand in Word documents. We also coded the student interviews for students' perspectives on the nature of their challenges and strengths as writers, the kinds of instructional support they found helpful, and their views on the effectiveness, or difficulty, of the think-aloud-based assessment method.

Phase 2 analysis, because of the interactive nature of the assessment sessions, focused primarily on the mediation that teachers provided students through their questions and prompts, and the students' responses to this mediation. For this coding scheme, we adapted a system created to capture teacher and learner "mediational moves" in dynamic assessment of language learning (Poehner, 2008) and writing (Shrestha & Coffin, 2012). Our adaptation required the revision and addition of many codes to capture the unique nature of the think-aloud assessment data. As with dynamic assessment of language learning, think-aloud writing assessment involved in-person, face-to-face interactions—which the existing dynamic writing assessment research, based on email exchanges and teacher comments on student papers, did not. The codebook developed for this phase is represented in Appendix B. Codes for teacher and student moves were applied in Dedoose qualitative software, and we used this software to explore patterns of mediational moves across students and teachers. We also read the transcripts inductively to identify segments of the assessment sessions that seemed particularly productive in terms of solving students' composing problems or of eliciting students' agency as writers. The codes for aspects of writing developed for Phase 1 of the research were used to tag segments of the interaction identified as particularly salient, for the reasons just mentioned. Inter-rater agreement on the coding scheme was assessed through a combination of iterative calculations of agreement and resolution of disagreements through discussion.

Table A.1. Codes for aspects of writing

Code	Definition
Analyzing/Interpreting/ Synthesizing	Challenges in the higher-level thinking skills associated with the writing task
Audience Needs	Challenges in satisfying the imagined reader's needs
Cohesion	Challenges in keeping the ideas in the piece together
Evaluating	Challenges in evaluating the quality of the writing
Fulfilling Task Demands	Challenges in doing what the task required
Generating	Challenges in generating ideas
Goal-Setting	Challenges in setting goals
Graphomotor Abilities	Challenges in the physical requirements of writing
Internal Focus	Challenges in keeping focused due to a wandering mind
Interpreting Task Demands	Challenges in figuring out what the task required
Introduction/Conclusion	Challenges in writing introductions and/or conclusions
Length	Challenges in writing a certain length of text or for a certain amount of time
Managing Writing Processes	Challenges in keeping track of all the processes at work in writing
Memory	Challenges remembering a piece of information
Pacing	Challenges in completing a piece of writing within the time allotted
Revising	Challenges in the revision process
Structuring	Challenges in structuring the writing
Topic Choice	Challenges in finding a topic
Topic Engagement	Challenges in being engaged in what one is writing about
Translating	Challenges in rendering one's ideas in the conventions of written English
Writing Environment	Challenges with the surrounding environment
Writing Off-Topic	Challenges in keeping the writing on topic

SUMMARY OF THE FINDINGS

Phase 1

Not surprisingly, most of the new information that teachers gained when listening to and observing their students thinking aloud while writing had to do with the writing process. For example, when teachers assessed only students' writing, they made no inferences about students' evaluating processes, their memory, their ability to focus, or their ability to manage their writing process. Yet teachers made inferences about all of these aspects of the writing process when they used think-aloud writing assessment. The number of inferences they made about almost all other aspects of the writing process when they used think-aloud assessment was twice the number they made when they evaluated only students' writing. Findings also showed that when teachers observed and listened to students thinking aloud in think-aloud writing assessment, they were less likely to characterize students based on traits such as intelligence, persistence, diligence, language proficiency, or perceived level of engagement in class. Teachers also were more likely to notice students' strengths as writers when the teachers used the think-aloud approach, which appeared to be especially useful for revealing strengths in relation to what Flower and Hayes (1980) called "defining the rhetorical problem." Findings also showed that the ESL teachers in the group tended to make more inferences related to language—specifically the "translating" code in Table A.1 —and fewer inferences related to discourse aspects of composing, such as structuring the essay or defining the rhetorical problem.

Both ESL and ELA teachers noticed qualitative differences between the discourse students wrote in their essays and what they verbalized during their composing processes. For the ESL students, the differences had to do with sophistication of language, whereas for the ELA students the differences had to do with complexity of ideas.

With respect to what teachers learn about instruction when they listen to students think aloud, we found that teachers' instructional priorities had more to do with features of students' writing than with their writing processes. Specifically, the teachers set instructional priorities related to the structure of students' writing far more often than for any other aspect of their writing or for their writing process. However, when teachers gained visibility into students' composing processes through listening to them think aloud, the teachers did set more instructional priorities for certain aspects of process—specifically, planning, revising, and translating—than they did based only on evaluating students' writing.

Phase 2

When we analyzed the data from the interactive think-aloud assessment sessions, we found a recurring pattern of what we came to call "pivot points," moments that occurred when a teacher asked a question that had a dual function: on the one hand appearing to elicit assessment information while at the same time also prompting the student to move forward in the composing process and in some cases also to resolve a problem. The teacher move that most frequently triggered a pivot point was "checking understanding." This is a code that we employed to capture questions in which the teacher either (a) checked students' understanding or interpretation of the source text, or (b) checked their understanding of how an element of the text they had composed worked within the text. The effect of this move, in the case of pivot points, was typically to prompt the student to verbalize some knowledge that he or she was then able to apply in composing the essay. While there were some grade-level differences in the benefits that students reported receiving from teacher support, we also noticed that students across the five classrooms reported benefits in certain key areas of academic writing—namely, analysis, self-assessment, focusing, and planning.

Teacher and Student Moves in Think-Aloud Writing Assessment

Teacher Mediational Moves	
Code	**Definition**
Accepts a response	Teacher accepts or agrees with a student's ideas
Checks understanding	Checks student understanding of source text, author background or rhetorical/literary concepts
Praise/Encouragement	Expresses positive or encouraging sentiments about students' work
Elicits ideas	Asks for students' plans, thinking, or authorial intentions
Reflects or recalls	Reminds students of something they said or wrote earlier, or says back an utterance to emphasize it
Content clues	Uses a content clue (e.g., literary term) to scaffold students' thinking
Checks mutual understanding	Checks that the student and teacher have the same understanding, or elicits clarification
Metalinguistic clues	Guides students to think strategically about choices regarding any aspect of written discourse (vocabulary, grammar, rhetorical or narrative tactics)
Assessment question	Asks questions about students' general writing process
Provides one solution	Gives students solutions related to their own writing
Recast	Accepts student's idea but recasts it in different language
Comprehension support	Asks a question or makes a suggestion to support literal comprehension

Student Reciprocal Moves	
Code	**Definition**
Exemplifies, illustrates, or explains a concept	Gives an example, illustration, or explanation of a concept/phenomenon
Direct instruction	Shows or tells the student what to do or how to do something
Identifies or explains a problem	Identifies or explains a problem
Locates part of text needing improvement	Indicates a problem area in the text or composing process
Provides multiple solutions	Offers several solutions for consideration
Prompts to compose	Prompts the student to write
Prompts rereading	Prompts the students to reread what they have written, or the prompt
Sentence scaffolding	Provides a sentence stem or frame
Rejects the response with explanation	Rejects a student response and explains why
Rejects the response without explanation	Rejects a student response or idea without explaining why
Checks affect/motivation	Asks a question or comments on a student's mood/affect
Responds to student affect/behavior/gestures	Responds to a student's mood, facial expression, gestures
Prompts task clarification	Prompts the student to clarify what the writing task is
Prompts to verbalize	Prompts the student to think aloud
Asks learner to identify the problem	Notes that there is a problem but asks learner to find it
Student Reciprocal Moves	
Code	**Definition**
Asks for task clarification	[Self-explanatory]
Unresponsive	Usually a pause after which the teacher restates a question or tries another prompt

Student Reciprocal Moves	
Code	**Definition**
Expresses doubt or a lack of confidence	[Self-explanatory]
Identifies or explains the problem	"Problem" refers to a problem in the student's or composing process
Expresses uncertainty about what to focus on	[Self-explanatory]
Student hesitates to compose	[Self-explanatory]
Student composes	[Self-explanatory]
Incorrect or insufficient response to teacher's question	Gives an answer but it's wrong or insufficient
Correct or sufficient response to teacher's question	Gives a correct answer
Unable to answer a teacher's question or respond to teacher's prompt	Doesn't give any answer at all or says "I don't know"
Shows uncertainty about a concept	Concepts include: understanding of source text, characteristics of author, or rhetorical/literary concepts
Asks a metalinguistic question	Refers to questions about rhetorical tactics, narrative tactics, literary devices, the nature of literary fiction, or narrative strategies
Directly asks for support, content or technical	Involves asking for definitions of concepts, or questions about source text or author background
Rejects the teacher's support with explanation	Disagrees with teacher suggestion or refuses to answer question, followed by a reason
Rejects the teacher's support without explanation	Disagrees with teacher suggestion or refuses to answer question, without a reason
Recasts teacher's comment or suggestion	Accepting teacher's general idea but recasts it in different language
Evaluates teacher's support	More than just accepting or rejecting teacher support; student explicitly evaluates quality/usefulness of support

Teacher Mediational Moves	
Code	**Definition**
Accepts the teacher's suggestion or solution	Also refers to incorporating teacher feedback, or finishing a sentence stem the teacher provides
Chooses one of the solutions that the teacher provides	[Self-explanatory]
Imitates the teacher's language	[Self-explanatory]
Expresses positive affect	[Self-explanatory]
Resolution of a problem or achievement of a goal	Eureka moment; may or may not be in response to a teacher move
Self-assesses	Student (1) evaluates own work, (2) describes what he or she is attempting to do in the paper, or (3) describes typical writing process. This is a more general code than "Identifies or explains the problem" and should be used only when that code does not apply
Verbalizes conceptual understanding	Demonstrates understanding of topic or text, or genre knowledge
Verbalizes planning/generating	Articulates ideas for the essay
Gesture or behavior that elicits a reaction from teacher	For example, student uses spell check, opens a web browser to look something up, deletes a paragraph
Stops verbalizing or mumbles	[Self-explanatory]

Overview of Classrooms
Teachers, Students, and Writing Tasks

Students	Writing Task/Prompt
	Ms. Miller, Grade 9
Carmen Darius Diana	**Question:** Who should be the next leader of Rome now that Julius Caesar is dead? **Source text:** Shakespeare's *Julius Caesar* **Requirements:** • Write a persuasive speech addressing the people of Rome. • Use "TIEDIED" format for supporting paragraphs. • Introduce quotations ("E" in TIEDIED format) with the 5 Ws: who, what, where, when, why.
	Ms. Schnader, Grade 10
Leslie Dorinda Amanda Hannah	**Prompt:** Write a well-developed, text-based response of *four to five paragraphs*. In your response, identify a central idea in the text and analyze how the author's use of one writing strategy, *characterization*, develops this central idea. **Source text:** Shakespeare's *Othello* **Requirements:** • Identify a central idea in the text. • Analyze how the author's use of characterization develops this central idea. • Use strong and thorough evidence from the text to support your analysis (at least *three* quotes). • Use proper citation format of (Act.Scene.Line) after quotes: for example (2.3.15–16) • Organize your ideas in a cohesive and coherent manner. • Maintain a formal style of writing. • Follow the conventions of standard written English.

Students	Writing Task/Prompt
Ms. Stanley, Grade 12	
Laura Ramona Julia	**Questions:** Why are there so many references to "what is to become" of Eliza? Trace these references throughout the play. What broader concern for society might Shaw be expressing? **Source text:** George Bernard Shaw's *Pygmalion* **Requirement:** • Make explicit reference to the play, considering not just the what, but the how and the why of Shaw's choices.
Mr. Almador, Grade 11	
Prakash Leila Alynda	**Prompt/Question:** Identify F. Scott Fitzgerald's view of the American dream as communicated in *The Great Gatsby*. Describe the tone and mood of the text and explain how the author uses archetypes and symbols to communicate its philosophical message. OR F. Scott Fitzgerald's novel focuses on the male characters, but he has several clearly delineated archetypal female characters as well, each with her own desires, motivations, and needs. Write an essay comparing and contrasting Daisy Buchanan, Myrtle Wilson, and Jordan Baker. Ultimately, what is Fitzgerald's message to the reader about women and feminine power? **Requirement:** • Provide clear and accurate examples and evidence from the text and analyze by using insightful commentary and criticism.
Mr. Tancredi, Grade 12	
Alex Cameron Alisa	**Questions:** One of the major themes of Coleridge's "The Rime of the Ancient Mariner" is retribution: punishment for an action that violates morality or law. In the poem, how do the supernatural elements exact retribution? How do these elements develop the theme? **Requirement:** • Remember to cite evidence from the text.

Students	Writing Task/Prompt
	Mr. Clarkson, Ms. March, Mr. Binder, Ms. Collazo, and Ms. Lindner, All Grade 10
Alisha Malik Parwiz Fatima Simon Eva Jason Greg Andrew Maria Linda Daniel Barbara Janet Simone	**Prompt:** Think about a book or a movie that you read or saw recently. If a book, it may be a book that you are reading or have read recently in class. Write an essay in which you explain why this is a good book to read or movie to watch. Think about the reader of your essay as someone you want to persuade to read the book or watch the movie. Provide reasons to support your argument. **Requirements:** • Clearly state what makes the book or movie the best you have ever read or seen. • Provide details from the movie or book to show why it is the best. • Check your writing for correct grammar, spelling, and punctuation. • Organize your essay clearly.

References

Alavi, S., & Taghizadeh, M. (2014). Implicit/explicit mediations on L2 learners' internalization of writing skills and strategies. *Educational Assessment, 19*(1), 1–16.

Allen, D., Ort, S., & Schmidt, J. (2009). Supporting classroom assessment practice: Lessons from a small high school. *Theory into Practice, 48*(1), 72–80.

Andrade, H. (2010). Students as the definitive source of formative assessment: Academic self-assessment and the self-regulation of learning. In G. Cizek & H. Andrade (Eds.), *Handbook of formative assessment* (pp. 90–105). New York, NY: Routledge.

Andrade, H. G., Wang, X., Du, Y., & Akawi, R. L. (2009). Rubric-referenced self-assessment and self-efficacy for writing. *The Journal of Educational Research, 102*, 287–301.

Applebee, A., & Langer, J. (2011). A snapshot of writing instruction in middle schools and high schools. *English Journal, 100*(6), 14–27.

Bailey, A., & Heritage, M. (2008). *Formative assessment for literacy, grades K–6: Building reading and academic language skills across the curriculum.* Thousand Oaks, CA: Corwin/Sage Press.

Bakhtin, M. (1986). *Speech genres and other late essays* (V. W. McGee, Trans.). Austin, TX: University of Texas Press.

Bartlett, L., & Garcia, O. (2011). *Additive schooling in subtractive times. Dominican immigrant youth in the Heights.* Nashville, TN: Vanderbilt University Press.

Bass, J. A., & Chambless, M. (1994). Modeling in teacher education: The effects on writing attitude. *Action in Teacher Education, 16*(2), 37–44.

Beauvais, C., Olive, T., & Passerault, J. M. (2011). Why are some texts good and others not? Relationship between text quality and management of the writing processes. *Journal of Educational Psychology, 103*(2), 415–428.

Beck, S., Cavdar, D., & Wahrman, A. (2018). Learning to teach writing through dialogic assessment. *English Education, 50*, 4, 305–336.

Beck, S., & Jeffery, J. (2009). Genre and thinking in academic writing tasks. *Journal of Literacy Research, 41*, 228–272.

Beck, S., Llosa, L., Black, K., & Trzeszkowski-Giese, A. (2015). Beyond the rubric: Think-alouds as a diagnostic assessment tool for high school writing teachers. *Journal of Adolescent and Adult Literacy, 58*(8), 670–681.

Beck, S., Llosa, L., & Fredrick, T. (2013). The challenges of writing exposition: Lessons from a study of ELL and non-ELL high school students. *Reading and Writing Quarterly, 29*(4), 358–380.

Beck, S., Llosa, L., Black, K., & Anderson, A. (2018). From assessing to teaching writing: What teachers prioritize. *Assessing Writing, 37,* 68–77.

Beers, K. (2006). *When kids can't read: What teachers can do.* Portsmouth, NH: Heinemann.

Bereiter, C., Burtis, P., & Scardamalia, M. (1988). Cognitive operations in constructing main points in written argumentation. *Journal of Memory and Language, 27,* 261–278.

Bereiter, C., & Scardamalia, M. (1987). *The psychology of written composition.* Hillsdale, NJ: Erlbaum.

Berryman, L., & Russell, D. (2001). Portfolios across the curriculum: Whole school assessment in Kentucky. *English Journal, 90*(6), 76–83.

Black, P., & Wiliam, D. (1998). Assessment and classroom learning. *Assessment in Education: Principles, Policy and Practice, 5*(1), 7–73.

Bohlke, L. (1986). *Willa Cather in person: Interviews, speeches, and letters.* Lincoln, NE: University of Nebraska Press.

Boroujeni, S., & Shahbazi, M. (2011). The effect of instructional and motivational self-talk on performance of basketball's motor skill. *Procedia—Social and Behavioral Sciences, 15,* 3113–3117.

Bowles, M. (2008). Task type and reactivity of verbal reports in SLA: A first look at a task other than reading. *Studies in Second Language Acquisition, 30,* 359–387.

Bowles, M. A. (2010). Concurrent verbal reports in second language acquisition research. *Annual Review of Applied Linguistics, 30,* 111–127.

Britton, J. (1970). Talking and writing. In E. Everetts (Ed.), *Explorations in children's writing* (pp. 21–32). Urbana, IL: National Council of Teachers of English.

Britton, J., Burgess, T., Martin, N., McLeod, A., & Rosen, H. (1975). *Development of writing abilities (11–18).* London, UK: Macmillan.

Brookhart, S. (2011). Educational assessment knowledge and skills for teachers. *Educational Measurement: Issues and Practice, 30*(1), 3–12.

Brown, J. S., Collins, A., & Duguid, P. (1989). Situated cognition and the culture of learning. *Educational Researcher, 18,* 32–42. doi: 10.3102/0013189X018001032

Caldwell, J., & Leslie, L. (2010). Thinking aloud in expository text: Processes and outcomes. *Journal of Literacy Research, 42,* 308–340.

Chi, M.T.H., de Leeuw, N., Chiu, M.-H., & LaVancher, C. (1994). Eliciting self-explanations improves understanding. *Cognitive Science, 18,* 439–477.

Ciofalo, J. F., & Wylie, C. (2006). Using diagnostic classroom assessment: One question at a time. *Teachers College Record, 108*(1). Retrieved from http://www.tcrecord. org/PrintContent.asp?ContentID=12285

Cizek, G. (2010). An introduction to formative assessment: History, characteristics and challenges. In G. Cizek & H. Andrade (Eds.), *Handbook of formative assessment* (pp. 3–17). New York, NY: Routledge.

Collins Block, C. (2003). *Literacy difficulties: Diagnosis and instruction for reading specialists and classroom teachers* (2nd edition). New York, NY: Pearson.

Cosner, S. (2011). Teacher learning, instructional considerations and principal communication: Lessons from a longitudinal study of collaborative data use by teachers. *Educational Management, Administration and Leadership, 39*(5), 568–589.

Cumming, A. (1989). Writing expertise and second-language proficiency. *Language Learning, 39*(1), 81–141.

Cummins, J. (1984) *Bilingual education and special education: Issues in assessment and pedagogy.* San Diego, CA: College Hill.

Datnow, A., & Hubbard, L. E. A. (2015, April). Teachers' use of assessment data to inform instruction: lessons from the past and prospects for the future. *Teachers College Record,* 117, 1–26.

Davin, K. (2013). Integration of dynamic assessment and instructional conversations to promote development and improve assessment in the language classroom. *Language Teaching Research, 17*(3), 303–322.

De La Paz, S., & Graham, S. (2002). Explicitly teaching strategies, skills and knowledge: Writing instruction in middle school classrooms. *Journal of Educational Psychology,* 94, 291–304.

Duff, P. (2010). Language socialization into academic discourse communities. *Annual Review of Applied Linguistics,* 30, 169–192.

Dufour, R. (2004). What is a professional learning community? *Educational Leadership, 61*(8), 6–11.

Durst, R. (1987). Cognitive and linguistic demands of analytic writing. *Research in the Teaching of English, 21*(4), 347–376.

Dutro, E., Selland, M. K., & Bien, A. C. (2013). Revealing writing, concealing writers: High-stakes assessment in an urban elementary classroom. *Journal of Literacy Research, 45*(2), 99–141.

Dweck, C. (2006). Mindset: The new psychology of success. New York: Ballantine

Ebner, R., & Ehri, L. (2013). Vocabulary learning on the internet: Using a structured think-aloud procedure. *Journal of Adolescent and Adult Literacy, 56*(6), 480–489.

Elbow, P. (1973). *Writing without teachers.* New York, NY: Oxford University Press.

Elbow, P. (1981). *Writing with power.* New York, NY: Oxford University Press.

Elbow, P. (1987). Closing my eyes as I speak: An argument for ignoring audience. *College English, 49*(1), 50–69.

Emig, J. (1971). *The composing processes of twelfth graders.* Urbana, IL: National Council of Teachers of English.

Englert, C. S., Raphael, T., Anderson, L., Anthony, H., & Stevens, D. (1991). Making strategies and self-talk visible: Writing instruction in regular and special education classrooms. *American Educational Research Journal, 28*(2), 337–372.

Erickson, F. (2007). Some thoughts on "proximal" formative assessment of student learning. *Yearbook of the National Society for the Study of Education, 106*(1), 186–216.

Ericsson, K. A. (2003). Valid and non-reactive verbalization of thoughts during performance of tasks. *Journal of Consciousness Studies, 10*(9–10), 1–18.

Ericsson, K. A., & Simon, H. A. (1993). *Protocol analysis: Verbal reports as data.* Cambridge, MA: MIT Press.

Ewert, D. E. (2009). L2 writing conferences: Investigating teacher talk. *Journal of Second Language Writing, 18*(4), 251–269.

Fisher, D., & Frey, N. (2003). Writing instruction for struggling adolescent readers: A gradual release model. *Journal of Adolescent and Adult Literacy, 46,* 5, 396–405.

Flower, L., & Hayes, J. (1980). The cognition of discovery: Defining a rhetorical problem. *College Composition and Communication, 31*(1), 21–32.

Flower, L., & Hayes, J. (1981). A cognitive process theory of writing. *College Composition and Communication, 32*(4), 365–387.

Fox, E., Dinsmore, D., & Alexander, A. (2010). Reading competence, interest, and reading goals in three gifted young adolescent readers. *High Ability Studies, 21*(2), 165–178.

Fox, M., Ericsson, K. A., & Best, R. (2011). Do procedures for verbal reporting of thinking have to be reactive? A meta-analysis and recommendations for best reporting methods. *Psychological Bulletin, 137*(2), 316–344.

Fry, S., & Griffin, S. (2010). Fourth graders as models for teachers: Teaching and learning 6+1 trait writing as a collaborative experience. *Literacy Research and Instruction, 49*(4), 283–298.

Fu, D. (2009). *Writing between languages: How English language learners make the transition to fluency, grades 4–12.* Portsmouth, NH: Heinemann.

Gillespie, A., Graham, S., Kiuhara, S., & Hebert, M. (2014). High school teachers' use of writing to support students' learning: A national survey. *Reading and Writing, 27,* 1043–1072.

Gillet, J. W. & Temple, C. (2000). *Understanding reading problems: Assessment and instruction* (5th edition). New York, NY: Longman.

Graff, N. (2009). Approaching authentic peer review. *English Journal, 9*(5), 81–87.

Graham, S., Harris, K., & Hebert, M. (2011). *Informing writing: The benefits of formative assessment: A Carnegie Corporation Time to Act report.* Washington, DC: Alliance for Excellent Education.

Graham, S., & Perin, D. (2007). *Writing next: Effective strategies to improve the writing of adolescents in middle and high school.* New York, NY: Carnegie Corporation.

Graves, D. (1982). *Writing: Teachers and children at work.* Portsmouth, NH: Heinemann.

Grossman, P., Schoenfeld, A., & Lee, C. (2005). Teaching subject matter. In L. Darling-Hammond & J. Bransford (Eds.), *Preparing teachers for a changing world: What teachers should learn and be able to do* (pp. 201–231). San Fransisco, CA: Jossey-Bass.

Grossman, P., Valencia, S., Evans, K., Thompson, C., Martin, S., & Place, N. (2000). Transitions into teaching: Learning to teach writing in teacher education and beyond. *Journal of Literacy Research, 32*(4), 631–662. doi:10.1080/10862960009548098

Hammill, D., & Larsen, G. (2009). *Test of written language—4th edition (TOWL-4).* Austin, TX: Pro-ed.

Hattie, J., & Timperley, H. (2007). The power of feedback. *Review of Educational Research, 77*(1), 81–112.

Hatzigeorgiadis, A., Zourbanos, N., & Mpoumpaki, S. (2009). Mechanisms underlying the self-talk–performance relationship: The effects of motivational self-talk on self-confidence and anxiety. *Psychology of Sport and Exercise, 10,* 186–192.

Haywood, H. C. (1992). Interactive assessment: A special issue. *Journal of Special Education, 26,* 233–234.

Haywood, H. C., & Lidz, C. (2007). *Dynamic assessment in practice: Clinical and educational applications.* New York, NY: Cambridge University Press.

Haywood, H. C., & Tzuriel, C. (2002). Applications and challenges in dynamic assessment. *Peabody Journal of Education, 77,* 2, 40-63, DOI: 10.1207/S15327930PJE7702_5

Heritage, M. (2008). *Learning progressions: Supporting instruction and formative assessment.* Washington, DC: Council of Chief State School Officers.

Heritage, M. (2010). *Formative assessment: Making it happen in the classroom.* Thousand Oaks, CA: Corwin.

Hillocks, G. (2002). *The testing trap: How state writing assessments control learning.* New York, NY: Teachers College Press.

Hochman, J., & Wexler, N. (2017). *The writing revolution.* Hoboken, NJ: Wiley.

Holloway, D. (1981). Semantic grammars: How they can help us teach writing. *College Composition and Communication, 32,* 2, 205–218.

Hoogeveen, M., & van Gelderen, A. (2013). What works in writing with peer response? A review of intervention studies with children and adolescents. *Educational Psychology Review, 25,* 473–502. doi:10.1007/s10648-013-9229-z

Hoogeveen, M., & van Gelderen, A. (2015). Effects of peer response using genre knowledge on writing quality. *Elementary School Journal, 116*(2), 265–290.

Hull, G. & Rose, M. (1989). Rethinking remediation: Towards a social-cognitive understanding of problematic reading and writing. *Written Communication, 6,* 2, 139–154. doi: 10.1177/0741088389006002001

Juzwik, M. M., Borsheim-Black, C., Caughlan, C., & Heintz, A. (2013). *Inspiring dialogue: Talking to learn in the English classroom.* New York, NY: Teachers College Press.

Kibler, A. (2010). Writing through two languages: First language expertise in a language minority classroom. *Journal of Second Language Writing, 19,* 121–142.

Kiuhara, S., Graham, S., & Hawken, L. (2009). Teaching writing to high school students: A national survey. *Journal of Educational Psychology, 101*(1), 136–160.

Kymes, A. (2005). *Journal of Adolescent and Adult Literacy, 48*(6), 492–500.

Langer, G. M., & Colton, A. B. (2005). Looking at student work. *Educational Leadership, 62,* 5, 22–26.

Lantolf, J. (2009). Dynamic assessment: The dialectic integration of instruction and assessment. *Language Teaching, 42*(3), 355–368.

Lewis, C., Perry, R., & Murata, A. (2006). How should research contribute to instructional improvement? The case of lesson study. *Educational Researcher, 35*(3), 3–14. doi:10.3102/0013189X035003003

Lytle, S. (2008). Practitioner inquiry and the practice of teaching: Some thoughts on "better." *Research in the Teaching of English, 42*(3), 373–379.

Magnusson, S., Krajcik, J., & Borko, H. (1999). Nature, sources and development of pedagogical content knowledge for science teaching. In J. Gess-Newsome & N. Lederman (Eds.), *Examining pedagogical content knowledge* (pp. 95–132). Dordrecht, The Netherlands: Kluwer Academic Publishers.

Marshall, J. D. (1987). The effects of writing on students' understanding of literary texts. *Research in the Teaching of English, 21,* 30–63.

McCarthey, S. J. (2008). The impact of No Child Left Behind on teachers' writing instruction. *Written Communication, 25*(4), 462–507.

McKeown, R., & Gentilucci, J. (2007). Think-aloud strategy: Metacognitive development and monitoring comprehension in the middle-school second-language classroom. *Journal of Adolescent and Adult Literacy, 51*(2), 138–147.

Mehan, H. (1979). *Learning lessons: Social organization in the classroom.* Cambridge, MA: Harvard University Press.

Meskill, C. (2010). Moment by moment formative assessment of language development: ESOL professionals at work. In H. Andrade & G. Cizek (Eds.), *Handbook of formative assessment,* (pp. 198–211). New York, NY: Routledge.

Moss, P. (2003). Reconceptualizing validity for classroom assessment. *Educational Measurement: Issues in Practice, 22*(4), 13–25.

Murray, D. (1968). *A writer teaches writing* (2nd ed.). Boston, MA: Houghton Mifflin.

Murray, D. (1990). *Shoptalk: Learning to write with writers.* Portsmouth, NH: Heinemann.

National Council of Teachers of English/International Reading Association. (1996). *Standards for the English Language Arts.* Urbana, IL/Newark, DE: Author.

New York State Education Department. (2014). *Educator's guide to the 2014 Regents Examination in English Language Arts (Common Core).* Albany, NY: Author.

New York State Education Department. (2017). *New York State Next Generation ELA Learning Standards.* Albany, NY: Author.

New Zealand Council for Educational Research. (2012). e-astTTle writing (revised) Manual. Auckland, NZ: Ministry of Education. Available at http://e-asttle.tki.org.nz/content/download/1574/6323/file/e-asTTle%20writing%20(revised)%20Manual%202012%20(3).pdf

Newell, G. (1994). The effects of written between-draft responses on students' writing and reasoning about literature. *Written Communication, 11*(3), 311–347.

Newell, G. (1996). Reader-based and teacher-centered instructional tasks: Writing and learning about a short story in middle-track classrooms. *Journal of Literacy Research, 28*(1), 147–172.

Newell, G. E., Bloome, D., & Hirvela, A. (2015). *Teaching and learning argumentative writing in high school English language arts classrooms.* New York, NY: Routledge.

Nichols, S. L., & Berliner, D. C. (2007). *Collateral damage: How high stakes testing corrupts America's schools.* Cambridge, MA: Harvard Education Press.

Norman, K. A., & Spencer, B. H. (2005). Our lives as writers: Examining preservice teachers' experiences and beliefs about the nature of writing and writing instruction. *Teacher Education Quarterly, 32*(1), 25–40.

Nystrand, M. (1989). A social-interactive model of writing. *Written Communication, 6,* 66–85.

Nystrand, M. (1997). *Opening dialogue: Understanding the dynamics of language in the classroom.* New York, NY: Teachers College Press.

Olson, C., Scarcella, R., & Matuchniak, T. (2015). *Helping English learners to write: Meeting Common Core Standards, grades 6–12.* New York, NY: Teachers College Press.

Ortmeier-Hooper, C. (2013). *The ELL writer: Moving beyond basics in the secondary classroom.* New York, NY: Teachers College Press.

Pajares, F. (2003). Self-efficacy beliefs, motivation and achievement in writing: A review of the literature. *Reading & Writing Quarterly, 19*(2), 139–158.

Pappas, C., & Tucker-Raymond, E. (2011). *Becoming a teacher researcher in literacy teaching and learning*. New York, NY: Routledge.

Parr, J., & Timperley, H. (2010). Feedback to writing, assessment for teaching and learning, and student progress. *Assessing Writing, 15,* 68–85.

Patthey-Chavez, G. G., & Ferris, D. R. (1997). Writing conferences and the weaving of multi-voiced texts in college composition. *Research in the Teaching of English, 31*(1), 51–90.

Pella, S. (2012). What should count as data in data-driven instruction? Toward contextualized data-inquiry models for teacher education and professional development. *Middle Grades Research Journal, 7*(1), 57–75.

Poehner, M. E. (2008). *Dynamic assessment: A Vygotskian approach to understanding and promoting second language development*. Berlin, Germany: Springer.

Poehner, M. E., & Lantolf, J. P. (2010). Vygotsky's teaching-assessment dialectic and L2 education: The case for dynamic assessment. *Mind, Culture, and Activity, 17*(4), 312–330.

Poehner, M. E., & van Compernolle (2011). Frames of interaction in dynamic assessment: Developmental diagnoses of second-language learning. *Assessment in Education: Principles, Policy and Practice, 18,* 2, 183–198.

Pribram, K. H., Miller, G. A., & Galanter, E. (1960). *Plans and the structure of behavior*. New York, NY: Holt, Rinehart and Winston.

Rainey, E., & Moje, E. (2012). Building insider knowledge: Teaching students to read, write and think within ELA and across the disciplines. *English Education, 45*(1), 71–90.

Ruiz-Primo, M. A. (2011). Informal formative assessment: The role of instructional dialogues in assessing students' learning. *Studies in Educational Evaluation, 37*(1), 15–24.

Sachs, R., & Polio, C. (2007). Learners' uses of two types of written feedback on a L2 writing revision task. *Studies in Second Language Acquisition, 29*(1), 67–100. doi:10.1017/S0272263107070039

Santangelo, T., Harris, K., & Graham, S. (2007). Self-regulated strategy development: A validated model to support students who struggle with writing. *Learning Disabilities: A Contemporary Journal, 5*(1), 1–20.

Santangelo, T., Harris, K., & Graham, S. (2016). Self-regulation and writing: Meta-analysis of the self-regulation processes in Zimmerman and Risemberg's model. In C. MacArthur, S. Graham, & J. Fitzgerald (Eds.), *Handbook of writing research* (2nd ed., pp. 174–193). New York, NY: Guilford Press.

Sawyer, K. (2004). Creative teaching: Collaborative discussion as disciplined improvisation. *Educational Researcher, 33*(2), 12–20.

Schleppegrell, M. (2004). *The language of schooling*. Mahwah, NJ: Erlbaum.

Schleppegrell, M. (2007). The meaning in grammar. *Research in the Teaching of English, 42,* 1, 121–128.

Schneider, C. & Randel, B. (2010). Research on characteristics of effective professional development programs for enhancing educators' skills in formative assessment. In G. Cizek & H. Andrade (Eds.), *Handbook of formative assessment* (pp. 251–276). New York, NY: Routledge.

Schoenbach, R., Greenleaf, C., Cziko, C., & Hurwitz, L. (1999). *Reading for understanding.* San Francisco, CA: Jossey-Bass.

Schunn, C., Godley, A., & DeMartino, S. (2016). The reliability and validity of peer review of writing in high school AP English classes. *Journal of Adolescent and Adult Literacy, 60*(1), 13–23.

Shepard, L. (2000). The role of assessment in a learning culture. *Educational Researcher, 29*(7), 4–14.

Shepard, L. (2005). Formative assessment: Caveat emptor. Paper presented at the ETS Invitational Conference, *Formative Assessment: Shaping the future of teaching and learning.* New York, NY: October 10–11.

Shrestha, P., & Coffin, C. (2012). Dynamic assessment, tutor mediation and academic writing development. *Assessing Writing, 17,* 55–70.

Shulman, L. S. (1987). Knowledge and teaching: Foundations of the new reform. *Harvard Educational Review, 57*(1), 1–23.

Silva, T. (1993). Toward an understanding of the distinct nature of L2 writing: The ESL research and its implications. *TESOL Quarterly, 27, 4,* 657–677.

Sisserson, K., Manning, C., Knepler, A., & Joliffe, D. (2002). Authentic intellectual achievement in writing. *English Journal, 91*(6), 63–69.

Slomp, D. (2008). Harming not helping: The impact of a Canadian standardized writing assessment on curriculum and pedagogy. *Assessing Writing, 13,* 180–220.

Smagorinsky, P. (1998). Thinking and speech and protocol analysis. *Mind, Culture, and Activity, 5*(3), 157–177.

Smagorinsky, P. (2011). *Vygotsky and literacy research: A methodological framework.* Rotterdam, The Netherlands: Sense Publishers.

Spence, L. K. (2010). Discerning writing assessment: Insights into an analytical rubric. *Language Arts, 87*(5), 337–347.

Stiggins, R. (2001). The unfulfilled promise of classroom assessment. *Educational Measurement: Issues and Practice, 20*(3), 5–15.

Stiggins, R., & Chappuis, J. (2009). Using student-involved classroom assessment to close achievement gaps. *Theory into Practice, 44*(1), 11–18.

Stratman, J. F., & Hamp-Lyons, L. (1994). Reactivity in concurrent think-aloud protocols. In P. Smagorinsky (Ed.), *Speaking about writing: Reflections on research methodology* (pp. 89–112). London, UK: Sage.

Supovitz, J. (2009). Can high-stakes testing leverage educational improvement? Prospects from the last decade of testing and accountability reform. *Journal of Educational Change, 10,* 211–227.

Topping, K., Buchs, C., Duran, D., & van Keer, H. (2017). *Effective peer learning: From principles to practical implementation.* London, UK: Routledge.

Tremmel, R. (2001). Seeking a balanced discipline: Writing teacher education in first-year composition and English education. *English Education, 34,* 6–30.

Valdes, G. (2001). *Learning and not-learning English: Latino students in American schools.* New York, NY: Teachers College Press.

Valli, L., & Buese, D. (2007). The changing roles of teachers in an era of high-stakes accountability. *American Educational Research Journal, 44*(3), 519–558.

van Compernolle, R., & Williams, L. (2012). Promoting sociolinguistic competence in the classroom zone of proximal development. *Language Teaching Research, 16,* 39–60.

van Compernolle, R., & Zhang, H. (2014). Dynamic assessment of elicited imitation: A case analysis of an advanced L2 English speaker. *Language Testing, 31*(4), 395–412.

van Gelderen, A. (1997). Elementary students' skills in revising: Integrating quantitative and qualitative analysis. *Written Communication, 14*(3), 360–397.

Vygotsky, L. S. (1978). *Mind in society.* Cambridge, MA: Harvard University Press.

Weissberg, R. (2006). Scaffolded feedback: Tutorial conversations with advanced L2 writers. In K. Hyland & F. Hyland (Eds.), *Feedback in second language writing* (pp. 246–265). Cambridge, UK: Cambridge University Press.

Wenger, E. (1998). *Communities of practice: Learning, meaning, and identity.* Cambridge, UK: Cambridge University Press.

Wiliam, D. (2010). An integrative summary of the research literature and implications for a new theory of formative assessment. In G. Cizek & H. Andrade (Eds.), *Handbook of formative assessment* (pp. 18–40). New York, NY: Routledge.

Williamson, P., Carnahan, C., & Jacobs, J. (2012). Reading comprehension profiles of high-functioning students on the autism spectrum: A grounded theory. *Exceptional Children, 78*(4), 449–469.

Wilson, M. (2007). Why I won't be using rubrics to respond to students' writing. *English Journal, 96*(4), 62–66.

Zimmerman, B., & Risemberg, R. (1997). Becoming a self-regulated writer: A social cognitive perspective. *Contemporary Educational Psychology, 22,* 73–101.

Index

About the Author

Sarah W. Beck is associate professor of English education at New York University. She has taught English in high schools in Boston and Ohio, and college-level writing at universities in Missouri and New York. These experiences inform her current work with high school teachers of English and literacy in all disciplines. Sarah aims to conduct research that directly contributes to students' literacy development while also cultivating teacher expertise.